MONEY
MANUAL

THE
MONEY
MANUAL

Everything You **Actually** Need to Know About Personal Finance

ABIGAIL FOSTER

EBURY EDGE

UK | USA | Canada | Ireland | Australia
India | New Zealand | South Africa

Ebury Edge is part of the Penguin Random House group of companies
whose addresses can be found at global.penguinrandomhouse.com

Penguin Random House UK,
One Embassy Gardens, 8 Viaduct Gardens, London SW11 7BW

penguin.co.uk
global.penguinrandomhouse.com

Penguin
Random House
UK

First published by Ebury Edge in 2025

Set in 13.5/16pt Garamond MT Std
Typeset by Six Red Marbles UK, Thetford, Norfolk

Printed and bound in Great Britain by Clays Ltd, Elcograf S.p.A.

The authorised representative in the EEA is Penguin Random House Ireland,
Morrison Chambers, 32 Nassau Street, Dublin D02 YH68

A CIP catalogue record for this book is available from the British Library

ISBN 9781529147032

Penguin Random House is committed to a sustainable future
for our business, our readers and our planet. This book is made
from Forest Stewardship Council® certified paper.

*To those of you who have ever been made to feel
inadequate when dealing with money.*

Contents

CONTENTS

PART FOUR

Managing your Money

PART FIVE

Building your Wealth

CONTENTS

Introduction

Money doesn't have to be intimidating. If you've ever felt overwhelmed by finance, you're not alone, and I get it. Every day as an accountant, I get asked the same questions over and over again, and it's not because people aren't switched on. It's because our system has failed to make financial knowledge accessible. So, rather than waiting for that to change, I decided to write this book for you.

They call me the woman with the best hair in finance – and no, those aren't my words! But it is funny since I come from a line of hairdressers. Growing up, I'd listen to conversations between my mum and her clients as she cut their hair. I learned the hairdresser ways early on and saw how people opened up to her, sharing their many problems and often secrets with her. The trust people placed in her was incredible. As I got older, the conversations got deeper. When I told these women I was going to do accountancy at university, the questions rolled in. 'What do I do with my taxes?' 'Should I be scared of this HMRC letter?' 'Where do I put my savings?' It was always the same answer when I asked why they didn't ask their own accountant. 'Oh gosh, no; they'll think I'm stupid, and I never understand what they say'. That was maddening. Education was clearly lacking.

I know now it's an 'everyone' problem, not just a hair client one. This realisation has informed everything I've done in my career to date, including this book. For too long, finance has been shrouded in complexity, only accessible to those who can afford expert advice or who happen to be in the right circles. The information is presented in ways that feel intimidating or alienating and I want to change that. This isn't just another jargon-heavy finance guide. It is a straightforward, no-nonsense approach to the core principles you actually need to grow your financial knowledge, feel confident with money and afford to get on with the life you want to live. None of the patronising fluff. Whether you're curious about budgeting, saving or even taxes, this is a space for you to learn without judgement or fear of getting it wrong. My goal with *The Money Manual* is to equip you with the tools and knowledge required to navigate the world of finance confidently. I want this book to eliminate the need for me, so you can become your own financial expert.

But let's rewind first.

I did go on to study accountancy at university. I started off working in practice. This means I was doing things like bookkeeping for various Mr and Mrs Smiths' accounts. Eventually, I was offered a management accountant job at Condé Nast, the publishers of *Vogue*. My sole focus became the magazine and its financial well-being. I later moved to Hearst, which publishes the likes of *Harper's Bazaar*, *Good Housekeeping*, *Women's Health* and *Men's Health*. I started to get more stakeholder time, and just like the women in my mum's hair salon, my colleagues had many questions about finance, particularly what their forecasts and projections actually meant. During my time at Condé Nast and Hearst I had to pass 15 exams to reach chartered accountant status. I wanted to give up constantly. Exams really aren't my thing. As someone with dyslexia, I find them to be the most stressful experience. But I committed to injecting as much fun as I could into the process. I turned up to every single exam (and quite a few resits – not everything hits the first time) in a bright pink Juicy Couture tracksuit. It became my lucky outfit. It was hilarious to see the faces of the invigilators and others around me. It brought me some joy in the process, and it has stayed with me; it's how I tackle things as a qualified chartered accountant now. The way to make finance accessible is to inject some joy and fun into the process, and to talk to people the way their hairdresser does.

Eventually, I left my 9-to-5 to start Elent, a financial education company that places fun and plain speaking at its core. I work with schools and businesses alike, but my heart belongs to the children I teach. Teaching seven- and eight-year-olds about money is a great way to strip things down to their essential nature. I got tired of hearing the same promise, year after year, that financial education would finally become part of the curriculum. 'It's definitely going to happen,' they said. And when I say 'they', I mean the people with the power to change it. I've sat in rooms with economic secretaries, asked the governor of the Bank of England and even sat down with a serving prime minister to advocate for a change in the curriculum. Every time, I hear the same answer: 'It's a great idea, but it's not realistic.' But why not?

The uncomfortable truth is it doesn't benefit those in power for the next generation to be financially confident. Imagine if every 18-year-old understood how to use a credit card wisely. Suddenly, the revenue for credit card companies would drop because they make money when people fall into debt, not when they manage it responsibly. I find it maddening that we spend years learning about tectonic plates but never how to renegotiate our salary. At school I was tested on how to use a compass – something I've never once needed – but nobody thought to teach me how to read my payslip.

That's why I started teaching. It became my mission to fill the gap that our education system refuses to address because real financial confidence comes from understanding the basics that no one bothers to explain. It turns out I'm good at explaining complicated concepts. Fast. My seven- and eight-year-old students have trained me well. This has allowed me to create and nurture an online following on social media. I now work with the likes of His Majesty's Revenue and Customs (HMRC), Downing Street, and the Bank of England so

I can explain to my audience what they are trying to get across in a way that anyone can understand. I've also picked up a Sunday morning radio slot on LBC, which I love, and you might see me on Sky News every now and then. Education is my mission. And that's where this book comes in.

I truly believe that financial literacy can change lives, not just for individuals but for society as a whole. Imagine a world where financial knowledge is common, where people understand the basics of budgeting, saving, investing and managing debt, no matter their background. Young people, in particular, would benefit immensely. Financial literacy would give them a sense of empowerment and independence, setting them up for happier, more secure futures. No more stumbling through early adulthood racking up debt or making uninformed decisions that could take years to recover from. They'd have the knowledge to make smart financial choices from the start, and that would ripple out into all areas of their lives. As a society, we'd see greater trust and understanding around money. Financial literacy would reduce the fear and confusion that often surrounds financial systems, leading to a more engaged and informed public. People would be less likely to fall for crappy financial products or scams and more likely to make decisions that benefit them in the long run. In very real terms, a financially literate society would also mean wealthier futures for everyone. By bridging the gap between 'excuses' and 'success' we can create a culture where financial stability and growth are accessible to all, not just a privileged few. Wealth would no longer feel like an unattainable goal for most people but something that can be built and sustained through informed intentional actions. That's the future. I get excited about the idea that we can shift financial knowledge from something exclusive to something empowering for everyone. It can be frustrating to see financial advice dished out by non-experts, often by influencers or content creators who have picked up bits of knowledge second-hand. Many of them focus on strategies that generate personal income for themselves rather than offering help that can genuinely build long-term wealth for others. This is not just misleading; it can be dangerous. Poor financial education can lead to risky investments, misunderstood tax obligations and long-term financial struggles. My contribution to the topic comes from a place of deep expertise which I want to put to your service.

It turns out that writing everything you know is quite tricky when you have a mind that is constantly distracted, but every time I sat down at my desk to write this book, I thought of you, the reader. The one who needs this book to take their own finances in hand so they can live the life they want. I won't let you down.

This book is for everyone. While I'm proud to be a woman in finance, the reality is that the financial system wasn't built to be inclusive. Historically, it was shaped by certain groups and didn't always reflect the needs of a diverse population. Women weren't widely welcomed into these spaces until the 1970s, but the truth is the system has been failing many people, men and women alike. But we have the power to change that. The financial system, as it stands, doesn't automatically serve everyone's needs, so we need to take charge and build the knowledge and resources necessary to create a financial future that works for all of us. That's what this book is about: helping you to understand how the system works so you can take control, make informed decisions and create the financial opportunities that will bring real, positive change to your life.

How to use this book

Take this book as the financial education you should have been taught at school, written up specifically for you by your best friend, who just also happens to be an accountant. Hi, best friend!

The book is divided into five parts, from understanding your money all the way through to building your wealth. We're going to start with the foundations. I know it's tempting to skip to the 'exciting' parts, like investing, but without solid foundations, your 'money house' won't stand the test of time. Along the way, we'll break down the topics you might not think are relevant, like who HMRC is, but everything has a place, trust me. At the end of each chapter, you'll find a summary to recap and refresh. If you're revisiting the book, these sections will serve as quick highlights. Scattered throughout, you'll also see 'Good to know' boxes which contain one-off snippets or links to resources where you can find more info. These bits might feel repetitive sometimes, but that's by design. We don't learn everything in one sitting; finance is an evolving skill that grows with repetition.

Please be aware that everything I talk about in this book is entirely educational, none of this is personalised advice and if you need that please seek out someone qualified – and who makes you feel great!

Let's get to work.

PART ONE
How to Understand Money

Money is more than just numbers in your bank account or cash in your wallet. It's a tool that influences nearly every decision we make, from our daily coffee runs to the long-term goals we set for ourselves. But genuinely understanding money, what it is, how it works and, most importantly, how we interact with it is something many of us struggle with. This is more than just a practical skill; your relationship with money can shape your opportunities, influence your stress levels, and ultimately determine the life you lead.

In these opening chapters, we're going to strip away the layers of complexity surrounding money and finance, beginning with a simple but often misunderstood distinction: what's the difference between money and finance? We throw these words around like they mean the same thing, but understanding the distinction is critical to mastering your financial future. One is a tool, the other is a system, and learning how they work together is your first step to gaining control.

Then, we'll shift the focus to something even more personal: your mindset around money. We all have a 'money story'. In this section, we'll explore how those experiences impact your financial decisions today and how you can shift your mindset to build healthier habits moving forward.

1. What's the Difference Between Money and Finance?

We all have this weird belief that it's not polite to talk about money. So we don't. The problem gets worse, and we never think of questioning whether the lack of conversation is giving others more power over us. To make matters worse, when financial institutions try to 'teach', it's always done in super patronising ways that aren't even remotely engaging or relatable.

I'm not saying understanding finance is always easy, but you definitely don't have to be an accountant or a financial advisor to understand what money is or how money works; you just need the right person to set it all out for you and explain what these things are and how they work for you. Don't forget, I'm your new best friend now.

I believe finance education is critical. We don't get to drive cars without tests; we even have probation periods when we start a new job. Yet, with finance, there's no formal learning path. We usually pick up bits of knowledge here and there, sometimes at school, perhaps around age 16 when student loans start to come up, but the majority of financial responsibilities only appear after we turn 18. Suddenly, we're eligible to take on debt, invest and access a range of financial products. Without proper guidance, we then rely on those around us; we are so used to learning from our teachers or friends or parents, and if that fails us, or they don't know the answers, which is more than often the case, we just avoid the subject altogether.

Financial education can empower you. Without education and knowledge, how do we know that we're doing the right thing? By the right thing, I mean specifically for you and your circumstances. People tell us what worked for them, but that isn't necessarily going to suit you and your circumstances. If you include elements like where you live, the job you have and the lifestyle you are looking to achieve, it can change the narrative you need to succeed.

In this chapter, we'll look at what money actually is, its recent history and its impact on you and your life.

What is money and how does it work?

Money is just an idea. We once bartered horses for wheat and wheat for wood, and so on; then we became sophisticated and created clay tokens. Then, many years later, we developed a receipt for storing wealth and, money rebranded to its most current 'look': the banknote.

According to the Bank of England (BOE), money needs to serve three purposes: it should be a store of value, meaning it retains its worth over time; a unit of account, so we can measure and compare the value of different things, whether it's gold, pounds, euros or dollars; and a medium of exchange, allowing us to easily transfer it to others with the confidence that it will be accepted and retain its value.

So what is cash?

Cash is built on trust. The British pound notes, famous for depicting royals and key figures on them, are a currency that our government has printed.

On these notes you will see the phrase 'I promise to pay the bearer the sum of [e.g.] ten pounds', signed off by the chief cashier, Sarah John (we'll get to where she works later), and we all go about our lives with complete faith in cash. I asked someone at the BOE if I could get myself on the next note, and they said you have to be dead to be on a note – sad times. British coins are minted (i.e. physically produced) by the government, and seals of approval are pressed into each one.

Our cash is a type of currency that isn't backed by a physical commodity, like gold or silver, but rather by the trust and authority of the government that issues it. It is a fiat currency. 'Fiat' means 'by decree', meaning the value of our money is based on the government's declaration that it has worth. This might sound weird, but it's actually how most modern economies operate.

This system gives governments flexibility to manage

their economies by controlling the money supply. However, it also means that the value of fiat currency is more sensitive to things like inflation, monetary policy and the general confidence people have in the economy. That's why if people lose trust in the currency or the government, the value of that currency and what it can buy vs. other currencies can decline rapidly.

So, it's essentially a tool of trust and convenience. We all agree that it has value, and we use it as a way to store, measure and exchange wealth. Without this collective agreement, that ten-pound note in your pocket is just a piece of paper. Fun fact: banknotes have been made out of polymer (plastic) since 2021, which helps keep them fresh and durable. It also has an accessibility benefit; the tactile bumps added to the notes help those who are visually impaired to identify them without losing their functionality over time.

What is income?

Even seven-year-olds can tell me when I'm in class that adults earn income through going to work. What work looks like is different for each of us, but they understand that going to work means getting paid.

That pay is called income: the income they receive for their work. You get work income from your job, but you can also gain investment income from investments you've made and self-employed income if you work for yourself.

What is the difference between money and finance?

Finance refers to the broader economic concepts and systems built around the use and management of money.

We know a transfer of money occurs for many around payday or their birthday, when they've done the month's work or hit another milestone, and they get paid, but what do government budgets or Profit and Loss statements fall under? That's when we get into the world of finance.

Think of finance as the management, movement and review of money and investing (which is technically money but sometimes in a different way from pounds and dollars). There are various specialisms within finance as well, such as personal finance, corporate finance for businesses, public finances (which are organised by institutions like HMRC) and even entire industries like financial services or investment management companies that manage finances for others.

Are maths and finance the same thing?

Back in 2018, there was an initiative called 'Maths Until 18.' The goal was to make sure students continued studying maths until they were 18 as part of a broader effort to raise educational standards and help the UK compete with other countries on employability skills. Many argued that this would lead to better financial literacy too. It may sound like a good idea on paper.

But does learning maths actually help us understand finance better?

The short answer is no. Maths and finance are not the same thing. Yes, they both involve numbers, but they operate in very different ways. If being good at maths gives you the confidence to feel more in control of your money, that's fantastic, but that's not the reality for most people. Finance is less about calculating angles with Sin-CosTan (remember that?) and more about making smart decisions with your money. Something that often has more to do with understanding value, risk and behaviour than advanced algebraic equations.

The truth is, you don't need to be a maths genius to be financially successful. So, while 'Maths Until 18' may have its merits, it's important to challenge the idea that being good at maths automatically translates to being good with money. In the real world, financial literacy involves a mix of practical knowledge, emotional intelligence and long-term planning, not just mathematical skills. It's about knowing how to make informed decisions about your spending, saving and investing, and how to navigate the systems that govern our financial lives.

Money and its recent history

Each generation has experienced money and finance in unique ways as economies shift with booms and busts.

While the 1980s and 1990s saw easier borrowing and high-interest mortgages on much smaller sums, today's buyers face lower interest rates but much larger loans. The 1960s brought credit cards, the 1970s stagflation and borrowing spikes, and the 1980s saw a surge in personal loans. We had the introduction of the National Lottery in 1994, transforming public funding, and in 1997 the Bank of England gained independence in setting interest rates that impact our savings and mortgage rates.

Fast forward to modern times, and the rise of digital-only neo-banks and cryptocurrencies (online decentralised currencies – see Chapter 13) has disrupted traditional banking.

Lifestyle ideals promised to us as young people, like owning a home, raising a family and attaining higher education, have become vastly more expensive and increasingly out of reach. Many of us are facing the reality of working far longer than previous generations, extending into what used to be considered retirement years. And that's another complex conversation we'll dive into later when we discuss pensions (Chapter 14). In short, retirement in the UK increasingly places the burden on the individual through workplace pensions; the state pension, a benefit that politicians can manipulate, may not even be available by the time many of us need it.

The way that we now consume is faster than ever. Ten years ago, if you wanted a pair of jeans that you saw in a magazine, you'd probably have to wait till Saturday, if not the last Saturday of the month, before you could go into town and buy the jeans. And that's only if the shops you went into that you could afford had that particular style. And they definitely didn't have the same ones that the model was wearing, but they might have something similar that made you feel like you look that little bit more like her. Now, with the rise of TikTok shops and sites like Shop LTK (a shopping platform that allows users to shop influencer-recommended products directly through their app, connecting brands with consumers via curated content), you can watch an influencer show an outfit that she's just bought and instantly purchase it yourself.

And this brings me to one of the biggest challenges we face today: the constant comparison we experience, especially on social media. Platforms like Instagram and TikTok bombard us with images of influencers showcasing extravagant lifestyles, luxury vacations, designer clothes and expensive cars – all of which create unrealistic expectations about what success looks like. It's easy to scroll through your feed and feel inadequate, as if you're failing because you don't live up to these curated, often unattainable standards.

This comparison culture is toxic, especially for young people still forming their sense of identity. Without a strong foundation in financial literacy, they can easily fall into the trap of spending money they don't have just to 'keep up'. Credit cards, buy-now-pay-later schemes and overdraft spending become coping mechanisms, pushing people further into debt as they chase a lifestyle that's far beyond their means. It's a vicious cycle, and the constant dopamine hits from social media keep many people locked into it.

This is why financial literacy is not just important, it's essential. It should be a prerequisite for young people before they graduate high school. They need the tools to navigate this environment, to understand the reality behind what they see online, and to make informed financial decisions that protect their future.

The statistics are not in our favour; buying a house and retiring comfortably, these 'picket fence' dreams, are increasingly out of reach. We are being held up against a metric that feels impossible to attain, and it's no wonder so many of us feel disillusioned.

I sit in rooms and teach 'how to buy a house' to 17-year-olds in towns where, even on good salaries over a 20-year period, they would struggle to afford a flat. How am I supposed to instil a sense of financial hope in their futures when they are faced with housing markets and job markets that don't seem to offer them the same opportunities as generations before?

And yet, despite all these challenges, we have a system that hasn't evolved. Our education system remains stagnant while our circumstances have wildly changed. Financial literacy among the youngest members of our society is nearly non-existent. Combine that with the effects of social media's comparison culture, and it's a recipe for financial trouble.

Some economists want you to believe the outlook is bleak, but a bit of understanding can make a huge difference. Money is not finite, and you're entitled to financial success just as much as anyone else. The first part of this book aims to give you a foundation in what money is, how it differs from finance, and how cash operates in today's world. From there, everything – pensions, investing and beyond – will start to make sense.

THINGS YOU NEED TO REMEMBER:

- Money is a tool based on trust used to store, measure and exchange value.

- Finance is the broader management and movement of money involving personal and public financial systems.

- Financial literacy goes beyond maths; it's about making informed choices, not just crunching numbers.

2. Understanding your Relationship with Money

Financial anxiety at an all-time high

Financial health and mental health are deeply inter-connected. Stress, especially financial stress, can lead to mental health challenges, and it's not something we openly discuss enough. Just like stress from any source, financial worries can take a toll not just on your mind but on your body as well.

Think about it: even when you know a bill is due or you owe someone money, there's always that little nagging thought in the back of your mind. Even if you have enough in your account, *Has the payment gone through? Did it leave enough for everything else?* This constant low-level anxiety keeps you from living fully in the moment and can lead to physical exhaustion. It wakes you up at 3am, and suddenly, you're too tired for the gym, reaching for quick, often unhealthy food options just to make it through the day. Over time, this becomes a cycle that wears you down, mentally and physically.

Today, with rising mortgage rates, fluctuating energy bills and economic uncertainty, financial anxiety is more common than ever. Fear, let's call it what it is, can hold you back, making it seem as if one wrong move could unravel everything. Small concerns begin to snowball into overwhelming stress. If we don't address these thoughts, they grow into a paralysing fear of making mistakes. This fear keeps you stuck, clouding your ability to make decisions and resulting in inaction.

While some financial fears are rational, many are not. The key is learning to recognise the difference, and that's where financial education becomes a powerful tool.

Habits to combat financial anxiety

We have already covered how social media has transformed how we perceive wealth. Twenty years ago, you might have compared yourself to people in your town or workplace. Now, you're measuring yourself against anyone, anywhere. A quick scroll can show you an influencer's second sports car or a celebrity's penthouse, making you feel inadequate in comparison.

But remember: social media is a highlight reel. Ask yourself if these influencers are helping or harming your relationship with money. Are they encouraging you to make financial decisions that fit your life, or are they nudging you to keep up with someone else's? When I started to use social media more for my business, I got sucked into the world of 'this person is doing better than me and therefore I'm failing'. I know now that a lot of that 'sparkle' was fake, but it took time to find that out.

Instead, use social media to instil habits to combat

financial anxiety. Turn Instagram into a 'virtual hype person'. Follow people who uplift you, those who inspire and educate you, and friends who make you feel good. Surround yourself online with voices that help you grow. Many wealthy business owners weren't born into money; they learned, hustled and built their success. Following them, reading their books (you might be reading one now) and listening to their podcasts can provide insight and motivation to achieve your own goals. If scrolling becomes an endless loop of comparison, leaving you exhausted or feeling compelled to 'doom spend', step back and rethink your feed.

Financial stress can show up in physical signs, too: insomnia, brain fog and irritability. But there are powerful ways to counter it, like education, self-care and even meditation. Take advice from people like author and creator Tam Kaur, who champions 'healthy spending'. While impulse buys and quick fixes like fast food might lift your mood momentarily, true well-being comes from investing in things that genuinely improve your life, whether that's nutritious food, books or experiences that bring lasting joy.

You need to give yourself space to be you and be extraordinary, and if you fill your headspace with money worries and stress, you don't give yourself the capacity to invent what you're destined to invent. It might not be the next light bulb, but it's incredibly difficult to be creative when financial fear looms over you.

One of the most impactful ways to reduce financial

stress is to build healthy money habits. Habits shape our daily actions and, ultimately, our outcomes. They're the difference between feeling in control of your finances or constantly playing catch-up. But here's the thing: building habits isn't instantaneous. It's a process, and understanding that process can empower you to stick to it.

Research shows it can take anywhere from 21 days to over a year to build a habit. Habits are the foundation of that freedom. Once they're established, they remove decision fatigue and mental clutter. Let's say you have an automatic habit of saving 20 per cent of your income: you'll no longer have to stress about whether you're saving enough. By automating this habit, you create mental space for what truly matters, pursuing your passions, building relationships, and finding joy in your day-to-day life.

I want to give you the tools to tackle financial fear head-on. It would be impossible to cover everything, but it will give you the foundation to build on. Whatever your dream, it needs strong financial foundations to support it, and this is where you start.

What is a money mindset?

Your money mindset is the way you think and feel about money; this forms much earlier than you might expect. Research from the Money Advice Service shows that by the age of seven, kids are already developing a financial mindset, and some even say it starts before then.[1] It's not just about learning how to count or understand numbers; it's about how we emotionally react to financial scenarios, our beliefs around saving, spending, and pretty much anything to do with money.

Kids absorb these attitudes from the adults around them. I see it all the time when teaching young children. They repeat phrases like 'money doesn't grow on trees' or 'we can't afford that', but it's not just the words; they pick up on the emotions behind them. Whether it's stress, scarcity or excitement, kids start forming their own beliefs about money based on what they see and hear at home.

These early impressions stick. By the time we reach adulthood, we've built a financial mindset without even realising it, and that mindset influences how we handle money throughout life. But here's the good news: just because you've grown up with a particular mindset doesn't mean you're stuck with it for ever.

Have you ever wondered why some people seem naturally good at managing money while others struggle, no matter how hard they try? Often, it comes down to the messages they absorbed about money growing up. It could be how their nan spoke about pocket money or how their dad approached cash. It's often the luck of the draw, based on where and how we were raised — but through financial education, those attitudes can change.

Sophie's story

Sophie, 25, is in her second job after completing an apprenticeship in fashion design. Growing up, money wasn't really discussed at home, but there was a strong belief that owning a home was the ultimate goal. To save for one was a badge of honour. Right now, Sophie is renting because her job in central Manchester makes it hard to commute from her family home.

Earning about £27k a year means Sophie takes home around £1,913 monthly (it was fun for Sophie to find out you don't just divide £27k by 12 months, but more on that in Chapter 6). After essentials, she puts about £150 each month into her 'house savings pot', echoing the financial values instilled in her by her parents.

Living in Manchester, Sophie's social circle has expanded. She meets up weekly for a spin class with Beth, a colleague who radiates confidence in her financial decisions.

One evening after class, Sophie and Beth were chatting on their way out about Beth's decision to open a second stocks and shares ISA, taking advantage of new rules that allow for more flexibility in investing. Beth explained how she was diversifying her investments to build a robust financial portfolio.

Sophie was intrigued. Until now, she had focused solely on saving for a house deposit, viewing it as her primary financial goal. Beth's perspective was refreshing and at odds with her approach. Sophie wasn't diversifying; on the contrary, she was putting everything in one basket.

'I used to think saving for a house was the only way forward,' Beth confessed as they settled into a nearby café. 'But investing opened up new possibilities for me. It's not just about one goal; it's about securing my future in multiple ways.'

Beth's words lingered with Sophie. She found herself increasingly curious about how investments worked and how they could help her achieve financial security beyond just owning a home.

The following week, Sophie asked Beth to explain more about her investment strategy. Beth patiently described her approach, highlighting the benefits of investing through a stocks and shares ISA. She explained how it allowed her to benefit from compound growth and offered tax advantages, which made her money work harder for her.

'Think of it as planting seeds,' Beth said. 'The more you plant and nurture them, the more they'll grow. It's about creating opportunities for your future self.'

Inspired by Beth's insights, Sophie decided it was time to expand her financial horizons. She began researching different investment options and the advantages of diversifying her savings. With Beth's encouragement, Sophie felt empowered to take the first step.

I'll stop you there; in this story, you can see where we're heading. Sophie opens her own stocks and shares ISA; she might even then start to consider a self-invested personal pension (SIPP), or better yet, she remembers hearing something about her employer having to contribute to her workplace pension, and she contributes too. She doesn't need to have the same portfolio as anyone else, it's just about changing her mindset for the better.

The widening of your understanding and, in this case, Beth's understanding had a ripple effect that changed the outlook of Sophie's financial plans.

You might not be Sophie; you might be her friend Ed, who believes all debt is bad and refuses to even entertain the idea of getting a credit card. Or his brother Steve, who put his full junior ISA, which his parents had saved up, into cryptocurrency because it was the surefire thing.

Knowledge is power, and sharing it is very important. But your knowledge can also be led astray by deeply held beliefs that shape your money mindset. Your mindset is impacted by a whole host of influences. Now it's time to understand yours.

So, what mindset are you?

1. Scarcity mindset:
If you find yourself constantly worrying about not having enough, you might have a scarcity mindset. You may hold on to money tightly, avoiding any kind of financial risk. Perhaps people around you see you as cautious or even 'stingy', or maybe you're generous with others but can't bring yourself to spend on your own needs.

With a scarcity mindset, there's a constant fear that

money is always slipping through your fingers, never quite within your grasp. You might find yourself saying things like 'I'll never be able to afford that' or 'I'm never going to be rich.' This can feel like carrying around a weight, a persistent worry about money that overshadows other areas of life.

But this isn't about blame. It's just one type of mindset – and it's possible to shift it.

2. Abundance Mindset:

On the other end of the spectrum, an abundance mindset is marked by confidence in one's financial situation and a willingness to take calculated risks. You believe you can create wealth, and you are open to investing in your future. Honestly, this is where I hope to get you by the end of this book.

Now, that doesn't mean people with an abundance mindset feel carefree about every purchase. The difference is that those with an abundance mindset trust in their ability to create more wealth and see financial challenges as opportunities.

You'll hear this person say things like:

- 'There's always another way to create wealth.'
- 'I can afford to enjoy life while saving for the future.'
- 'Money flows easily and freely into my life.'

This last one might sound a bit 'woo-woo' but hang in there; I'll delve into that side of things later on.

3. Somewhere in between ...

One big difference between an abundance mindset and a scarcity mindset often comes down to whether you have a fixed or growth mindset. Carol Dweck popularised this concept, and it's pretty straightforward: a fixed mindset sees your financial situation as stuck like it's something you can't change. A growth mindset, on the other hand, believes that with effort and learning you can improve your situation. If you're open to learning and adapting, which, given you're reading this book, is most likely you, then there is room for growth.

So, how about we take a moment to check in to see where your mindset is right now? Take your time and go through steps 1 to 4 at your own pace. When you're ready, move on.

1. First, take a deep breath in, roll your shoulders back, and as you exhale, let them drop and relax. Now, close your eyes.
2. Picture money. What does it look like to you? Notice what feelings come up; are they positive or negative? Do you feel calm or tense?
3. Now, imagine what you want your relationship with money to look like. Can you see money flowing freely into your life? Do the numbers in your bank account bring you comfort or fear?

4. Once you've reflected, take another deep breath in and slowly let it out. Open your eyes and jot down your feelings about money now, as well as how you'd like to feel about it in the future.

The language we use

One of the most powerful habits you might have inherited is the way you talk about money. If you've ever caught yourself saying 'I'm just bad with money' or 'I'll never be able to afford that', these aren't just throwaway lines; they're reflections of deep-seated beliefs that can hold you back. The good news? These beliefs aren't facts, they're just habits of thought. And habits can be changed.

Start by being mindful of your language. Constantly speaking negatively about your finances reinforces limiting beliefs. It's not just what you say but *how* you say it and whether you truly believe it. Phrases like 'I can't' or 'I'm not good with this' create internal blocks, preventing you from exploring solutions or finding ways to improve.

Flip the script. Try saying 'I'm learning to be better with money' or 'I'm taking control of my finances.' Say it with conviction, and you'll slowly start to believe it. Belief leads to action, and soon enough you'll be surrounded by positive financial influences and find yourself dismissing negativity around money.

It's also important to recognise the financial history that may have shaped your mindset. Did you know that women in the UK are reported to not have been able to apply for a mortgage on their own until 1975[2]? Before that, a father or husband had to co-sign. Finance has traditionally been designed for a select few, with many, especially women, left out of the conversation for decades. This isn't your fault. If you feel any guilt or shame about your financial situation, remember that context matters. Understanding this history can help you let go of the emotional weight that often comes with money issues.

Your first money experiences have a lasting impact. If I asked you to tell me about your earliest memory of money, it might link closely to the way you view it now. In my role at Elent, I often get to work with young students, and junior school classes are some of my favourite days. Kids are like sponges, absorbing knowledge, and they also hype each other up with infectious positivity. When we discuss money, I start by asking them, 'What do you think about money?' The answers range from 'My parents have it' to 'I use money to buy sweets' to 'We don't have any.'

Their responses give me a great starting point. I can then adapt the conversation to challenge some of their inherited beliefs. I often think back to my younger self and wonder if, had someone challenged my own views on money sooner, I might have written this book at 20 instead of 30.

Is money different depending on your culture?

Absolutely.

From how we earn and spend to what we consider success and security, money is deeply woven into our personal and social identities, often shaped by cultural norms, traditions and societal expectations. In the UK, there's a historical blueprint of 'how things are done' when it comes to money, but it's essential to recognise that we're a society of many cultures and perspectives. Understanding how culture and money interact gives us insight into our financial habits and broadens our view on managing money.

In Kenya, Harambee means 'all pull together', reflecting community support similar to crowdfunding, while in West Africa and the Caribbean, a sou-sou is a group savings system that helps members pool resources for big expenses.

Wedding customs, like Nigeria's money spraying and Japan's cash gifts, symbolise prosperity and support. In Islam, zakat is a mandatory charitable giving, underscoring the importance of generosity. Chinese traditions include giving cash gifts during the Lunar New Year, symbolising luck and fortune, but avoiding amounts containing the number four (which is considered bad luck). Even in the UK, finding a coin in Christmas pudding or from the Tooth Fairy ties money to luck and learning, while Greek beliefs associate an empty wallet with bad luck. Jewish tzedakah emphasises charity giving and financial literacy. These traditions highlight the intricate ways culture influences financial habits and priorities, reminding us of the shared human values behind our financial decisions.

Within Islam, there is a law that states prohibitions of interest, meaning traditional interest-bearing loans and savings accounts are not permissible; they should not have excessive uncertainty and not be investing in unlawful activities such as alcohol and gambling.

The main takeaway here is that while this book is designed to give you practical tools for managing money, it's also important to recognise that your cultural background, upbringing and personal experiences make you unique. You're not 'average', and neither are your financial needs.

Some of your beliefs and habits around money might differ from traditional norms, and that's OK. For example, if you're guided by faith to donate a percentage of your income to charity, the typical 50/30/20 rule (see Chapter 8) might not quite fit, and that's perfectly valid.

I bring these cultural perspectives into focus to broaden our understanding of 'financial success', which is different for everyone. Our individual definitions of financial well-being are shaped not only by our upbringing but also by where we come from, and embracing that diversity is part of building a healthy relationship with money.

Money practices to enhance your money mindset

To help you start building new money habits, I've created a list of four simple but effective daily practices. You might find yourself doing these every day or just touching on them when it feels right, but each is designed to strengthen your relationship with money.

Number 1: Be a great listener. Social media has made us all great at sharing what we know but less skilled at listening to what others are really saying. But listening is one of the most powerful tools you can develop, and it's a skill you can apply to your own financial journey. Let me explain.

When I'd rush to offer quick solutions to quick problems, I'd miss the deeper concerns. I've learned to stop and listen instead. At first glance, financial anxiety might look like it's just about money, like worrying over debt or bills. But when you listen carefully, it often reveals a deeper fear, such as feeling out of control or insecure about the future. By recognising those underlying worries, I could respond with advice that went beyond just fixing the numbers.

For you, being a great listener could mean asking yourself what's really behind your financial stress. Is it fear of making mistakes? A sense of falling behind others? Or maybe not knowing where to start? The same applies if you're helping a friend or partner with their money worries. Start by listening, not rushing to solve. By understanding what's really driving the anxiety, you'll find solutions that are not just practical but meaningful.

Number 2: Embrace positivity. There's a quote I love: 'Financial titans are unbreakable optimists.' The most successful people in finance aren't just skilled number-crunchers; they're visionaries who believe in their ability to create a better future. They're not relying on luck; they have faith in their work ethic, creativity, and resilience. Start each day with the optimism that you can solve your financial challenges and create the life you want. This positivity isn't just feel-good talk; it's a habit that trains your brain to focus on solutions rather than problems.

Number 3: Schedule a monthly check-in. At least once a month, set aside time to review your finances. Whether it's checking your savings, reviewing your expenses or planning for future goals, this habit keeps you in tune with your financial reality. It's easy to avoid looking at your bank account when you're stressed, but a regular review helps you stay proactive and catch small issues before they become big problems.

Think of it this way: when you avoid looking at your bank account because you're stressed, you're reinforcing a scarcity or avoidance mindset. Over time, that habit can leave you feeling even more disconnected and anxious. But when you carve out time to review your savings, expenses or future goals, you're actively creating a mindset of accountability and intention. It's a simple habit that helps you take charge, spot opportunities and catch small issues before they become big problems.

Number 4: Be a great teacher and talk about money. If you've learned something valuable, share it. Whether it's with a friend, a colleague or a younger family member, teaching others about money can deepen your own understanding and reinforce your progress. Teaching is powerful because it not only solidifies your knowledge but also empowers others. Financial literacy is something we can all pass along, helping each other build confidence and control over our finances.

By sharing what you've learned and cultivating positive habits, you can start building the financial confidence and control you need. These practices will not only help you feel more in control of your finances but also provide a unique joy in knowing you've helped someone else achieve their goals. The journey to financial confidence is a shared one, and these small steps will carry you and those around you toward a stronger financial future.

What does being good with money look like?

You've probably heard people label themselves as 'savers' or 'spenders', but being good with money is about something more: *focus.*

Understanding money and navigating financial concepts can sometimes feel overwhelming. Progress may seem slow, or goals might feel out of reach. But remember, small improvements each day add up. You don't need to devour this book in one go. I'd actually encourage you to pace yourself. Come back to it, revisit chapters, and keep adding to your knowledge bit by bit.

Improvement takes time, and finance itself is always changing. What we'll work on together here is building your confidence with the essentials, giving you tools to understand both the basics and the more complex aspects of finance while being prepared for inevitable changes along the way.

What is financial focus?

Financial focus is about being deliberate with your money. It means paying attention not just to where your money is going but actively managing how you earn, spend, save and invest it.

Financial focus makes a difference to more than just numbers; it can boost your confidence, reduce stress and give you more freedom to make choices that serve your life and goals.

What is financial success?

Financial success is different for everyone. The key is understanding what it looks like *for you*. To help clarify this, try creating a vision board to capture what financial success means to you.

There are two ways to approach this: virtually or physically. You can hop onto Canva or Word, adding images, words and ideas that represent your goals. Maybe it's a house you'd love to own, a dream holiday, or even a pair of boots you've been eyeing. Or perhaps it's broader: financial freedom, the ability to pursue your passions, or creating opportunities for others. These broader goals can reflect long-term aspirations that go beyond material possessions and focus on your desired lifestyle or impact on the world.

Your vision board isn't a 'one-and-done' thing. You'll likely want to update it periodically, maybe once a year or whenever your goals evolve. Personally, I like to refresh mine every few months. As I hit milestones, I add new aspirations.

Once you've got your vision board, it's time to set clear, actionable financial goals. Financial success isn't about having more money; it's about having a plan to use it wisely. Start by defining both short-term and long-term goals. Perhaps your immediate goal is paying off a credit card, while a long-term goal is saving for a house deposit. Break these down into manageable steps. If you're aiming to save £5,000 for a trip, work out how much to put aside each month to meet your goal in a set timeframe.

Be specific. 'I want to save' isn't enough. Instead, try, 'I want to save £2,000 by June,' and break it into monthly or weekly targets. Keep your goals realistic and give yourself achievable timeframes; focus on what you can do now and adjust as needed.

The aim of this book isn't to get you to a single number; it's to bring you closer to freedom, security and the ability to make choices that enhance your life. Your vision board, goals and consistent habits will help you build the life you're working toward.

While it's a cliché to say, 'The best time to plant a tree was 20 years ago. The second-best time is now,' the truth is that the best time to organise your finances is today. Regular check-ins prevent issues from escalating and keep you on track.

Natural times for a 'financial check-in' are at the start of the tax year or at the start of a new year. But there's also a new trend you might enjoy: finance dates. Take yourself out on a finance date; it can be as simple as a quiet night at home with a nice meal and a candle, reviewing your finances with a positive mindset. Money dates should be a positive experience. If you're in a rough headspace, tackling finances might feel overwhelming, but when you're in a good frame of mind, reviewing your finances can boost your outlook and give you control over your money.

You can schedule these dates weekly, monthly or quarterly. Review the past week, month or quarter and look forward. If there's a partner in your life, having these dates together can be invaluable. Combining finances isn't necessary for everyone, but being aware of each other's financial situations and goals is essential for shared financial success.

Ultimately, financial success isn't a single finish line;

it's an evolving journey. It's about setting goals, staying consistent and adapting as life changes. By focusing on your goals, taking action and reviewing regularly, you're building the financial freedom you're aiming for.

Remember, no goal is too big, and nothing is out of reach. It all starts with a clear vision and consistent steps forward. You're in control of your financial future, and I'm here to help you make it happen. Let's bring those dreams on your vision board to life.

In the next chapter, we'll explore the role of the government, the Bank of England, the Treasury and other institutions in shaping your financial landscape. We'll dive into how fiscal and monetary policies impact both personal and business finances, shedding light on taxes and inflation.

Understanding how these macroeconomic forces impact your finances will give you insight into the broader financial world and help you manage your money wisely, even in times of change.

THINGS YOU NEED TO REMEMBER:

- The way you think, feel and speak about money shapes your financial habits. Positive language and beliefs can empower you to take control of your finances.

- Define what financial success looks like for you, whether through a vision board or by setting specific, measurable goals. Regular check-ins and small steps can help you turn those dreams into reality.

- Building financial knowledge not only helps you but also those around you. Sharing what you learn strengthens your understanding and supports others in their financial journeys.

PART TWO
The Finance World

Welcome to Part Two of your financial journey! Here, we'll uncover the big players and core concepts that shape the financial world we live in. Ever wondered why the Bank of England often makes headlines, how HMRC decides the taxes we pay, or why prices seem to keep rising? This section will give you the answers.

We'll start by looking at the key institutions at the heart of the UK's financial system: the Bank of England, which influences interest rates and monetary policy; HMRC, the government's tax collector; and the Chancellor of the Exchequer, who directs the country's economic strategy. Understanding these institutions is essential to grasp how money flows through our economy and affects our daily lives.

Next, we'll dive into taxes, why we pay them, where they go, and the types you might encounter, from income tax to inheritance tax. Taxes may not be the most thrilling topic, but they're central to how our society operates, and knowing the basics can make managing your money a lot smoother.

Finally, we will move on to inflation and price changes, those sneaky factors that seem to make everything more expensive over time. We'll break down what inflation actually is, why it happens, and how it affects everything from your weekly shop to your long-term savings.

Let's dive into the institutions, taxes and trends that drive the money game!

3. The Institutions

Why focus on the institutions behind finance? Because so much of our financial world is shaped by these powerful players, the point where money meets government and where institutions influence the economic landscape we all navigate.

In this chapter, we'll explore the key players that impact your finances, often in ways you may not even realise. From government decisions that affect your wallet to the banks that hold and move your cash, understanding these institutions is essential. Their decisions impact your money, so knowing how they operate and who they are empowers us to hold them accountable.

We'll break down how the government influences everything from taxes to benefits. You'll see how institutions like HMRC, the Bank of England and Downing Street directly impact you, often with just a few decisions made behind closed doors. We'll also take a look at the role of banks, both the traditional ones and the newer digital disruptors, so you can see how they make money and why it matters to you.

Banks

The most obvious institution for a book titled *The Money Manual* is where we store our money: banks. But there's a lot more going on beneath the surface than most people realise – possibly because many of us were raised to believe that it's rude to talk about money. Spoiler alert: it's not. And guess what? Banks talk about it every day; that's how they operate and make money.

How do banks make money?

Banks make money using *your* money. When you deposit funds in a current or savings account, the bank doesn't just keep it in a vault. Instead, they lend it out in the form of loans, mortgages and credit cards, charging much higher interest rates than the interest they pay on savings. For example, you might earn 1–3 per cent interest on your savings while the bank charges someone else 5–7 per cent interest on a mortgage. This difference is one of the ways banks make their profits.

Then there are fees. Banks love fees. They charge for overdrafts, premium accounts with perks like travel insurance, and late payments, among others. These fees may seem small individually, but across millions of customers, they generate substantial revenue.

What's the difference between a bank and a building society?

Let's start with a quick distinction. Banks and building societies are similar in that they both offer savings accounts and mortgages, but there's a key difference: ownership. Banks are owned by shareholders and aim to make profits for them. Building societies, on the other hand, are mutual institutions owned by their customers (known as members). When you put your money into a building society, you're technically a part-owner, and profits are often reinvested back into the business rather than paid out to shareholders.

This member-focused model can have real advantages. For instance, building societies often provide more competitive rates on mortgages and savings accounts because they don't have to prioritise shareholder profits. On the flip side, they might not offer the same breadth of financial products, like credit cards or international banking services, so the best option for you will depend on your individual needs.

For a real-world glimpse into this, check out *The Bank of Dave*, a movie based on a true story about a wealthy Yorkshire man who tried to lend money to locals and faced pushback when he attempted to formalise it into a real bank. It's a reminder that while banks provide essential services, the system isn't always as fair as it should be.

What's new in banks?

Up until about 15 years ago, not a lot. You had a local branch, a bank manager and maybe a savings account for your Christmas shopping. But things have changed recently and dramatically with the introduction of neo-banks, the disruptors. These are banks that are built for the modern world: no high street branches, no physical cheques, just a sleek app and a focus on giving you more control over your money.

They're adaptable and innovative, and what I love most is that they were born in the era where if you're going to build something, like the apps they use as opposed to physical branches, you have to make sure it does good for the environment and the people it serves.

There is little room for error, and this can cause issues because some of these banks can't offer every product that the old-timers can because of scale. It takes time to build up to that. If you're OK with neo-banks giving you a killer app but not a mortgage all-in-one service, then you're fine.

When it comes to banks and most things in life, you don't really want all your eggs in one basket, so if you're using a neo-bank, that's great. You can also have another account with another old-timer and get the benefits they offer as well. That's totally fine.

Also, in the realm of 'what's new in banks' (at least in comparison to traditional banking institutions that have been going since the eighteenth century), are supermarkets.

They love a bit of diversification, so why not open a bank? When financial services are offered by supermarkets, their customers can have an end-to-end experience where they purchase their shopping with a card also owned by them.

Supermarkets entered the banking world to leverage their existing customer base, diversify their revenue streams and be competitive against other big supermarkets. They have also diversified into 'data' by having a store card that can tell them what you are purchasing; they sell that data on to their producers and use it to recognise trends in geographic locations. It seems like a good idea given you may already have some loyalty towards that brand, but be aware that many of these banks are now owned behind the scenes by larger banks, and as they get taken over, the offers and services change – sometimes for the better, but this is not a given.

Investment banks

When you think of investment banks, you might picture *The Wolf of Wall Street*'s Jordan Belfort on trading floors selling penny stocks, with yachts and complex financial deals. But while these institutions often evoke images of massive sums being moved around, in reality they do a variety of different things.

At their core, investment banks are financial powerhouses specialising in services for corporations, governments and other large entities. Unlike retail banks, which deal with individuals' savings, loans and mortgages, investment banks facilitate large-scale financial activities. They're the behind-the-scenes players that drive major economic shifts.

Their services include:

1. Helping companies and governments raise money: This could involve issuing stocks or bonds (see Chapter 13) or arranging loans from institutional investors. When you hear about a company 'going public' through an IPO (Initial Public Offering), it's often investment banks making that happen by pricing and selling the company's stock to investors.

2. Advising: Whether that's on mergers or acquisitions, they can act between two parties, assess the value of businesses, negotiate and eventually get a deal done.

3. Investing: Like traditional banks, investment banks make money through fees for their services. They may also invest their own funds to generate profits or manage investments on behalf of clients for a fee.

In essence, investment banks are the architects of big financial deals. They don't just store money, they also help create, manage and move wealth around the world. While their services might feel distant from daily life, their influence reaches us through the growth of businesses, the health of the economy and even the strength of the job market.

The Bank of England

Think of banks and the Bank of England (BOE), not as sisters or family members like many think they are, but as friends: they're happy to lend to each other and do, but they aren't the same.

Let's say the BOE is like the much older friend in their retirement years who has plenty of money; they're set for life and they've got the wisdom to give good suggestions and advice. Then think of the high street banks and building societies as young, hungry 30-year-olds; they aren't poor by any means but they might lean on their older friend to lend them money now and again. The BOE lends out at the base rate which is announced every nine weeks; that's not the rate the rest of us get.

To understand the BOE's role, it helps to revisit what money represents. Money acts as a unit of exchange, and its value relies on public trust. Every banknote in the UK is effectively a promise from the BOE – a promise we accept when we agree that this piece of plastic (just a reminder that our bank notes are made out of plastic, not paper) is worth £5, £10 or £20. On every note, you'll see a signature, most often from Sarah John. As the BOE's chief cashier, her role is to guarantee the credibility of our currency.

Historically, banknotes were simply receipts for deposited gold. The BOE, holding more than 400,000 gold bars (though only two belong to the bank itself), originally issued these receipts as proof of deposit rather than permanent currency. Over time, it became easier to trade these paper receipts than the actual gold, leading to the evolution of banknotes as we know them today.

Despite the declining use of cash, with only 14 per cent of UK payments made in cash, it remains vital for many. A significant portion of the population prefers cash transactions, and many rely on them. In the UK, 1.1 million adults, or 2.1 per cent of the adult population, do not have bank accounts: they are unbanked. These individuals depend on cash as they lack access to digital financial services.

The Bank of England is committed to ensuring the availability of cash as long as there is a need for it. Cash is an essential part of the payment framework, offering a choice and providing a safe, reliable and secure method of payment. This commitment includes producing banknotes that are difficult to counterfeit, ensuring the integrity of cash transactions.

The Role of the Monetary Policy Committee (MPC)

The Bank of England (BOE) includes a group called the Monetary Policy Committee (MPC), made up of nine members who meet every nine weeks. Their job is to set the Bank of England's base rate, which is the interest rate at which the Bank of England lends to high street banks. These banks, in turn, use this base rate to determine the rates they offer when lending to us, whether for mortgages, loans or other financial products.

The MPC is headed by Andrew Bailey (the governor); the other members are three deputy governors, the chief economist and four external members appointed by the Chancellor of the Exchequer in power at the time.

For years, the base rate was so low that it hardly impacted consumers directly, sitting at just 0.1 per cent. But in the not-too-distant past we saw highs of 11.1 per cent, which has real effects on everyday finances. For consumers, this increase means that borrowing costs, such as mortgage payments, loan interest and credit card rates have also risen. So, if you're borrowing money, you'll likely pay more in interest now than you would have done a few years ago. On the other side, savers may see higher returns on savings accounts as banks increase interest rates to align with the higher base rate.

Accessibility in finance

Accessibility in finance is about making sure that everyone, regardless of ability or background, can participate fully in the financial system. The addition of tactile dots to modern UK banknotes (none on the £5, two on the £10, three on the £20 and four on the £50) might seem like a small detail, but for those with visual impairments, it's a game-changer. The simple act of identifying the value of your cash, something most of us take for granted, can now be done independently. And this is just one of many small but vital steps towards building a financial system that works for everyone.

Beyond physical currency, voice-activated banking and screen readers are transforming digital accessibility. Voice-activated services enable people with limited mobility or vision to manage their finances just by speaking, while screen readers convert on-screen text to speech, allowing visually impaired users to navigate online banking tools. These changes are small steps toward a more inclusive financial system where everyone can check balances, pay bills and transfer funds without barriers.

The BOE also makes headlines when there are changes in leadership or updates to banknotes, like the recent release of notes featuring King Charles III. Although these updates may seem ceremonial, they often indicate shifts in the broader financial landscape.

And beneath the BOE lies one of its most fascinating features: its gold vaults. Hidden beneath London, the vault contains around 400,000 gold bars – each weighing 12.5 kilograms – representing roughly £200 billion in value. This vast reserve is not just for show; it underscores the BOE's role as a foundational pillar of trust and stability in the UK economy. If you ever visit the BOE Museum, you can even try lifting a genuine gold bar; it's surprisingly heavy, much like the bank's influence on the financial world!

The government

How does the government impact your finances? In short, in almost every way. From benefits for new parents and pensioners to the taxes we pay, nearly every financial decision is influenced by government policy. Think back to the pandemic, when the government borrowed at record levels (second only to the world wars) to pay the wages of more than 9 million furloughed workers. This monumental intervention shows just how intertwined our economy is with the decisions made in Parliament.

The government's role is to manage risk, collect revenue and redistribute funds to keep the economy running for everyone. Sometimes they get it right, sometimes not, but from HMRC to Downing Street, an entire machine of institutions is at work shaping our financial landscape.

In this section, we'll examine key players like the Chancellor of the Exchequer and the processes that affect your wallet, from tax policies to national budgets. By the end, you'll have a clearer understanding of how government decisions influence your paycheque, savings and financial future.

The King's speech and the government's agenda

When a new government takes office, one of the first major events is the King's speech, a ceremonial moment when the monarch outlines the government's agenda for the coming year. It's a grand occasion steeped in tradition (the King's crown even gets its own carriage!) but it's more of a 'heads-up' than a concrete plan.

The King's speech gives a preview of upcoming policies, but the Chancellor is the one who turns these plans into actionable policies. The real financial impact emerges later, through the spring budget and the autumn statement, moments when policies turn into specific numbers that influence taxes, public services, and the broader economy.

His Majesty's Revenue and Customs (HMRC)

His Majesty's Revenue and Customs, or HMRC, is the government department that oversees one of the least-loved aspects of adult life: taxes. As an accountant, I've spent more time than I care to admit waiting on the phone with HMRC. But recently, I've had the chance to work with them on some pretty important stuff, like campaigns around child benefit and breaking down the spring budget into easy-to-understand content for everyone on social media, which is a place none of us expect to see HMRC, but I'm so glad they are there.

At its core, HMRC is responsible for collecting the taxes that keep the country running. Whether it's income tax, VAT or even inheritance tax, they're the ones making sure the government has the funds it needs to pay for everything from the NHS to education. They also handle various benefits, like child benefit, tax credits and grants, so it's not all about taking your money; they're also helping those who need it.

They get a bad rep for long phone waiting times and taking taxes. But here's the thing: they don't set the rules. Think of them as the finance department of the UK government; they enforce the tax policies, but they're not the ones making the big decisions. Those come from the Chancellor of the Exchequer and Parliament. HMRC is just there to carry out the plan.

For most of us, HMRC pops up whether we like it or not. You'll interact with them if you're self-employed and filing a tax return, receiving benefits or dealing with inheritance matters.

They also offer some relief and support, although they don't shout about it nearly enough. And while they might feel like a faceless bureaucracy, they're the ones working behind the scenes to make the government's financial plans a reality.

So, next time you hear about the spring budget or the autumn statement, remember that once the Chancellor stands up and lays out their vision, HMRC is the department that makes it all happen. They're an essential part of how money moves around in the UK, whether it's filling potholes, paying teachers or, yes, collecting your taxes.

Good to know: The acronym HM is also at the start of other areas of government, such as HM Treasury, His Majesty's Treasury.

HM Treasury

HM Treasury, also known as His Majesty's Treasury, is the UK government's economic and finance ministry. Think of it as the central hub that manages the country's money, from setting budgets to funding essential services. While HMRC is responsible for collecting taxes, HM Treasury decides how to spend it. It is responsible for balancing the books, managing public debt, and ensuring the government has enough resources to fund everything from healthcare and education to infrastructure projects.

One of the Treasury's key activities is also preparing the national budget, presented by the Chancellor of the Exchequer during the spring budget and autumn statement. The Treasury evaluates economic trends, forecasts growth, and allocates funds to different departments. When the government needs to borrow money, it oversees the issuance of government bonds (IOU's to investors).

Although it may seem distant from everyday life, decisions made by HM Treasury directly affect your finances and its role in shaping fiscal policy makes it one of the most powerful institutions in the UK's financial system.

The Chancellor of the Exchequer

The Chancellor of the Exchequer is the government's financial chief – the person who wields the famous red box (which, not to brag, I've held for a spring budget social media reel!). This role is based at 11 Downing Street, where the Chancellor devises the financial policies that are then presented to Parliament and ultimately influence your money.

You might hear a lot about the spring budget and autumn statement. These are crucial moments where the Chancellor lays out plans that affect everything from taxes and public spending to inflation and the national debt. For most people, these decisions shape the financial landscape, whether it's changes to income tax, the benefit system or beer duty, which is a tax applied to beer based on the strength of the drink.

For instance, if the Chancellor adjusts income tax rates or thresholds, your take-home pay changes immediately. Or if they cut funding for public services it could mean fewer resources for education, healthcare or transport. This stuff matters, and it's not just abstract numbers or political jargon. It directly influences your everyday life.

In recent years, the autumn statement has evolved from a minor update into a major event in its own right, especially post-COVID and after political moments like Liz Truss's brief term as prime minister. Both the spring budget and autumn statement now play essential roles, with policy changes that can directly affect your finances. When these statements are announced, look out for reliable analyses that break down key points into accessible information, whether from financial news sites or experts online. (I hear one of them has particularly great hair.)

The Chancellor also plays a critical role in crisis management. Think back to the pandemic, when furlough schemes, business grants and tax relief were all decisions made by the Chancellor. These measures helped keep the economy afloat during one of the most challenging periods in recent history.

But beyond managing crises, the Chancellor is responsible for long-term financial planning. Decisions on infrastructure, healthcare, education and innovation investments may not pay off immediately, but they shape the future, affecting job markets, housing opportunities and quality of life for generations to come.

Yes, the theatrics of booing and jeering in Parliament during budget announcements can be off-putting, but they shouldn't distract from the fact that these decisions affect everyone in the UK. While the system can seem frustrating, understanding it helps you stay informed and engaged with your finances To encourage the next generation to actively engage with their finances and the political landscape, it's essential to foster a culture of respect and accountability around these processes. This means holding those in power accountable for transparency and fairness and also encouraging young people to educate themselves on how decisions are made so they feel empowered to contribute and advocate for their own financial futures.

To stay financially informed, keep an eye on the spring budget and autumn statement announcements, usually around April and October. And remember, voting plays a big role in shaping these policies. The government runs for re-election roughly every five years, and despite what you might hear, your vote does matter. Deciding who represents you in Parliament can have a direct impact on your financial future.

From the grandeur of the King's speech to the concrete decisions of the Chancellor in the spring budget and autumn statement, these governmental forces shape the UK's financial landscape and influence our everyday finances. We've looked at HM Treasury and HMRC, the operational hubs of public finance, which are responsible for managing spending and collecting taxes.

With a clearer understanding of these institutions, it's time to shift our focus to a topic that affects us all: taxes. In the next chapter, we'll dive into why we pay taxes, how the system functions, and the essentials of self-assessment and inheritance tax. Equipped with this knowledge, you'll feel more prepared to manage your finances and navigate the tax system with confidence. Let's get into it.

THINGS YOU NEED TO REMEMBER:

- Decisions made by institutions like the Bank of England, HMRC and the Chancellor directly impact your taxes, savings and borrowing costs.

- The Bank of England's Monetary Policy Committee reviews the base rate every nine weeks, influencing everything from mortgage rates to savings interest.

- While HMRC collects taxes and administers benefits, it doesn't create tax policy, that's up to Parliament and the Chancellor. Think of HMRC as the financial engine that makes government plans a reality.

4. Tax

In the UK, we have taxes for a whole host of things, and the best way I've found to illustrate the tax system to six-year-olds and pensioners alike is this. We have subscriptions to Netflix and Disney+, right? I'll pretend you're nodding. Well, to live in the UK, you're effectively subscribing to live here.

You pay a monthly fee to Netflix, and in return, you expect *Bridgerton* on tap; you expect *The Office* (the US version, obviously ...), and this transaction just happens. To live in the UK and use the benefits like street lights and the NHS, we have to pay.

Now, taxes might not be the most thrilling topic, but they're far more relevant to your finances than most people realise. From income tax taken straight from your paycheque to the VAT added to your morning coffee, taxes are everywhere. And understanding how they work can help you make better financial decisions, from choosing investments to managing your take-home pay.

In the UK, the 'big three' taxes – income tax, national insurance (NI) and value added tax (VAT) – make up the bulk of government revenue. You probably interact with all three regularly, whether you notice it or not.

But there's much more to taxes than just the basics.

The goal of this chapter is to empower you, helping remove fear or uncertainty around taxes. By the end of the chapter, you'll feel equipped to handle your taxes with confidence and understand how they impact your finances at every stage of life.

Why do we pay taxes?

Taxes are the government's primary way of raising money, a system that has evolved and become quite creative over the centuries. Historically, taxes were often introduced to fund wars or even to curb certain behaviours, like excessive spending on luxuries. For example, the infamous window tax, which led to a weird backlash where people started bricking up their windows. Not surprisingly, it didn't last!

Here's why tax matters: taxation isn't just about taking money from people; it's about redistributing that money where the government thinks it's needed. The government is trying to balance paying for public services like healthcare, education, infrastructure and social support while also trying to keep the economy moving.

The 2023/24 national accounts revealed that the UK raised around £915 billion in tax revenue. Income tax, national insurance and VAT alone contributed £264 billion, £172 billion, and £162 billion, respectively, together making up nearly two-thirds of the total. This shows just how much of our tax revenue comes from these three sources alone.

Good to know: William Pitt, the youngest prime minister in British history, introduced income tax during King George III's (you know, the one in *Bridgerton* and *Hamilton*) reign to fund Britain's war efforts. Initially, it only applied to those earning more than £60 a year, a considerable amount back then. Although unpopular, the tax was essential and was eventually reinstated in the twentieth century.

Whether we realise it or not, the bulk of tax revenue (over 60 per cent) is drawn from taxes on employment. These employment taxes directly influence our take-home pay, our financial decisions and, ultimately, our lifestyle.

Employment taxes

Income tax and national insurance fund public services and social support systems. The way they're structured and applied can be a bit complex.

Let's start with income tax, which in England, Wales and Northern Ireland is split into three bands: the basic rate (20 per cent from £12,571 to £50,270), higher rate (40 per cent from £50,271 to £125,140) and additional rate (45 per cent over £125,140). Up to your personal allowance (currently £12,570), you pay no income tax, and beyond that, tax is applied in increasing percentages based on your earnings.

One element of income tax that often catches people off guard is the so-called '60 per cent trap' due to the tapering of the personal allowance. Introduced by Alistair Darling in 2009, this tapering creates an effective 60 per cent tax rate for those earning between £100,000 and £125,140. Here's how it works: once your income exceeds £100,000, you start to lose your personal allowance, which is the portion of your income that's tax-free. For every £2 you earn above £100,000, you lose £1 of this allowance. By the time you reach £125,140, your entire personal allowance is gone, leading to an effective tax rate of 60 per cent within this income range. Many people are unaware of this trap, but strategies like increasing pension contributions (don't worry, I will get to pensions in Chapter 14) can help mitigate it.

For some context, the top 1 per cent of income earners, those making over £190,000 a year, pay 30 per cent of all income tax. Meanwhile, the top 50 per cent of earners contribute 90 per cent of the income tax revenue.

To confuse matters a little bit there are also devolved countries in the UK, which can be in charge of their own laws (to an extent). What this means is that Scotland's income tax looks slightly different from that of England, Wales and Northern Ireland.

In Scotland, there is something called a starter rate of 19 per cent, which comes into play at £12,570. Then there is a basic rate of 20 per cent from £14,877 to £26,561, intermediate rate of 21 per cent from £26,562 to £43,662, higher rate of 42 per cent from £43,663 to £75,000, advanced rate of 45 per cent from £75,001 to £125,140 and top rate of 48 per cent over £125,140.

National insurance (NI)

National insurance originated in the early twentieth century and was initially designed as a form of social insurance, ensuring financial support for people in times of need. Both employees and employers contribute to national insurance, which initially funded benefits like healthcare, unemployment support and state pensions. The idea was simple: everyone pays in, creating a safety net to support individuals during life's unexpected events.

Originally, it was structured as a flat-rate contribution, meaning everyone paid the same amount, regardless of income, and received flat-rate benefits in return.

Over time, however, national insurance has evolved and now functions much like a general tax. It no longer exclusively funds the NHS or state pensions but is pooled with other tax revenues to finance a wide range of public services. Despite these changes, national insurance remains an integral part of the UK's social welfare framework, helping to protect individuals financially throughout their lives.

Self-employment taxes

If you're self-employed, or even if you have a side hustle, welcome to the world of self-assessment. Unlike traditional employment, where your employer handles taxes through Pay As You Earn (PAYE), with self-assessment, you're responsible for reporting your earnings and ensuring the correct tax is paid.

Self-assessment means exactly that: you assess your own income and calculate the tax you owe (although there is a handy HMRC self-assessment tool to help work that out). Even if you're employed and paid via PAYE, you may still need to complete a self-assessment form if you have additional income sources, such as freelance work, rental income or substantial investments.

The form we use is the SA100. It sounds a little intimidating, but here's the good news: the system has improved massively in recent years. There was a time when you had to trawl through pages of paperwork and remember every tax rule by heart just to avoid a fine. Now, HMRC has an online system that helps you by prefilling much of the information, making the whole process far smoother.

As a self-employed person, you still need to pay income tax, just like an employed person does. However, national insurance works a bit differently for self-employed individuals, with various 'classes' depending on your earnings. Fortunately, when you fill out your self-assessment form online, it will handle the calculations for you, showing exactly what you owe.

One of the best perks of being self-employed is that you can deduct allowable expenses from your income, meaning you only pay tax on your profits. These are costs that are essential to running your business, like office supplies, travel costs (not your commute, but things like business trips) and even utility bills (if you work from home, you can claim a portion of your heating, electricity and broadband).

HMRC has guidelines on what you can and can't claim, so keeping receipts and records throughout the year is essential. When it's time to file your return, typically at the end of January for self-assessment, you'll be prepared and won't risk being caught out.

People often ask, 'What if I mess up my self-assessment? Will I go to prison?' The short answer is no. HMRC isn't in the business of locking up people who make a mistake on their first SA100. If you make a genuine error, you might get a slap on the wrist with a 'please do better next time' letter or, at worst, a fine. But people who consistently and fraudulently report false earnings could face prison time.

How do I get a tax refund?

If you've overpaid tax during the year, HMRC will issue a refund automatically once your self-assessment is processed. Receiving a refund is a bit like finding £20 in an old coat pocket: always a pleasant surprise! However, it's best to aim to pay the correct amount from the start rather than rely on getting a refund later.

Business tax

When we talk about business tax, most people immediately think of corporation tax. This is the tax paid on a company's profits, but let's be clear: it's ultimately the people within those businesses, the business owners, who feel the impact of this tax. The OECD (Organisation for Economic Co-operation and Development) has even ranked corporation tax as the most harmful to economic growth because it can discourage investment and innovation.

As it stands, the corporation tax rate varies depending on the size of the business, with rates often fluctuating in line with government economic strategies. For instance, it used to be a flat percentage for all limited companies, and now it is based on earnings. It's a key area where businesses, especially small ones, are constantly trying to minimise their burden while still growing.

Another essential business tax is VAT, which is applied to goods and services at the point of sale. Originally known as 'purchase tax', VAT can be complex because different items are subject to different VAT rates, and not everything qualifies for VAT. Businesses registered for VAT must charge this tax on their sales once they exceed HMRC's income threshold.

VAT rates vary depending on the type of item. For example, goods considered luxuries, like chocolate-covered biscuits, are taxed at 20 per cent, while essential items, such as plain biscuits, are exempt. One famous case involved Jaffa Cakes: after much debate in court, they were classified as cakes rather than biscuits, making them exempt from VAT.

Inheritance tax (IHT)

There are more than 20 different types of taxes, so beyond employment and business taxes, you'll likely encounter others, and one that comes up as a tax many wish they learned about before they had to encounter it is inheritance tax.

To be honest, I end up discussing inheritance tax more than I'd like, whether with friends or even complete strangers, and I often find myself playing the big sister role. It can be one of the toughest parts of my job, sitting down with people and guiding them through the complexities of inheritance tax. I know it's not a topic they want to talk about, but in most cases no one has explained it to them before.

In a book about money that is all about empowering you, it can feel really odd to see a chapter on what happens once you're gone, but this tax worries many, whether they have a tax liability or not, and I wish I could hand these people a few pages on what to know and what comes next so here are those pages, from me to you.

Inheritance tax is actually only paid by 6 per cent of the UK population, and yet it has been declared the most hated tax in Britain. So how does it work? The tax itself is 40 per cent of anything over your allowances – not 40 per cent of the entire estate.

An estate is the total value of someone's assets and belongings at the time of their death. This includes everything they own, including property, money, investments, personal possessions and even certain types of trusts or gifts.

The allowances you're entitled to are a nil rate band (NRB) threshold, an amount you can have in your estate before you are taxed, currently standing at £325,000. This is for every single person in the UK. If your estate falls under £325,000, you can pass on all of that to whoever you like. If you have a property within your estate worth up to £500,000, you are entitled to the residence nil rate band (RNRB) of £175,000, meaning your estate could be about £500k before it gets taxed. The property must be in the estate when the person dies and must be passed to direct descendants. These allowances have been frozen for years, and unfortunately that means that because of rising house prices, many people are dragged into paying inheritance tax and don't realise it.

There's also the marriage allowance, which means if you're married to your partner, your entire estate transfers are entirely tax-free, and the £500,000 allowance also transfers to them. When your spouse passes, those allowances can be combined, and those that inherit your estate get £1 million of allowance for your estate.

Probate, which is the legal process of validating a will and distributing assets, typically takes some time. However, under the direct payment scheme, it's possible to sell off certain assets and use the proceeds to pay HMRC directly. This can be especially useful for covering tax liabilities on illiquid assets, which can be investments or properties that aren't easily converted to cash.

You can opt to pay inheritance tax in instalments to reduce the initial tax charge due at the six-month mark. These instalments are spread over ten years, with equal payments, though interest is charged daily on any unpaid balance. For example, if there's a £100,000 inheritance tax bill, the first instalment of £10,000 is due at the six-month anniversary. You could then continue to pay £10,000 plus interest annually until the full amount is covered. Alternatively, if you're able to raise funds later on, you could pay off the remaining balance in full at any point to avoid additional interest costs.

Probate is the document that unlocks the estate. It proves that the executor has the authority to deal with the estate, enables all the assets to be encashed, and proves that you've got the authority to sell the estate.

One way to start reducing the amount of your estate that is taxable is called gifting. This gets really technical, and as with everything, please seek out personal tax advice. The standard rule is that you can gift £3k to someone each year.

When it comes to gifting, the seven-year rule often comes up in conversations about IHT. Here's how it works: if you give away assets and live for at least seven years afterwards, those gifts are exempt from IHT. This is a great way to potentially reduce the taxable value of your estate. However, if you pass away within those seven years, things get a bit more complicated. The amount of IHT due on the gift starts to 'taper' after three years. This means that the longer you live after making the gift (up to seven years), the less tax your beneficiaries will have to pay. The rule is designed to prevent people from giving away all their assets on their deathbeds to avoid tax, ensuring that the system remains fair for everyone. So, if you're planning to make significant gifts, it's worth considering the seven-year rule as part of your estate planning strategy.

There are also some 'rogue' exemptions, like agricultural and business property relief, which can offer some inheritance tax relief on qualifying assets, such as farmland or trading businesses, providing valuable opportunities for those in certain industries.

Pension Exemptions

Your pension currently falls outside of your estate for IHT purposes, although there are changes coming for inherited pensions that will fall part of the estate. If you pass away before the age of 75, your pension can be transferred tax-free to your chosen beneficiary. After 75, it's subject to income tax when withdrawn, but not IHT. To ensure it goes to the right person, make sure you complete an 'expression of wishes' form.

THINGS YOU NEED TO REMEMBER:

- Income tax bands, like the '60 per cent trap' and national insurance contributions, vary based on income, affecting take-home pay.

- Self-employed individuals manage taxes via self-assessment, allowing for deductions on business expenses, while businesses are taxed on profits through corporation tax.

- Inheritance tax is levied on estates above certain thresholds, with options like the seven-year rule for gifting to reduce taxable amounts.

5. Inflation and Price Rises

Coming off the back of our deep dive into taxes, it's time to tackle a topic that impacts our wallets every day: inflation. You've probably heard about inflation on the news, seen it discussed on social media or even felt its sting. Your weekly shop seems to cost more, your rent has gone up and your savings don't seem to stretch as far as they used to. That's inflation for you. It isn't just an abstract concept discussed by economists; it's something that affects all of us, no matter our income or financial situation.

We'll examine what it is, how it impacts you and what you can do to protect yourself from inflation's effects. Whether it's investing wisely, saving smarter or just being aware of your spending habits, there are ways to manage inflation and lessen its impact on your financial health. This chapter will arm you with the knowledge and tools you need to better understand and ultimately survive the inevitable price rises that inflation brings.

What is inflation?

Inflation is a backwards-looking metric released monthly by the Office for National Statistics (ONS). It refers to the general price increases that have happened in the last year on a basket of goods and services. When you hear people talking about inflation being 'high' or 'low', they're referring to how much more expensive goods and services have become over the past 12 months.

The BOE aims to keep inflation at around 2 per cent. Why 2 per cent? It's considered the 'sweet spot' for economic stability. At this rate, prices rise steadily enough to keep the economy growing but not so fast that your savings lose value overnight or your paycheque doesn't cover what it used to. A moderate inflation rate encourages people to spend and invest, knowing that money won't sit idle and lose value. On the flip side, it's also slow enough that we don't see runaway price increases, which could lead to chaos.

Our friend Mr Bailey at the BOE uses tools like adjusting the base interest rate to control inflation. If inflation exceeds the 2 per cent target, the bank might raise interest rates. Higher interest rates make borrowing more expensive, which can slow down spending and investment, helping cool off inflation. On the other hand, if inflation dips below 2 per cent, the bank may lower interest rates to encourage people to borrow and spend more, stimulating the economy.

It's a delicate balancing act: too much inflation can erode the purchasing power of your money, while too little can stall economic growth. While 2 per cent is the goal, recent events have shown us that inflation can swing well beyond that target, making it a major focus for anyone trying to manage their finances.

How is inflation calculated?

There are several ways to measure inflation, with terms like CPI (consumer price index), CPIH (consumer price index including owner occupiers' housing costs) and RPI (retail price index) commonly mentioned. Here's a breakdown of what each one means and why they're important.

First up is CPI. This is probably the one you've heard the most about. CPI tracks the prices of more than 700 goods and services that represent what an 'average' person in the UK buys – a basket of everyday items, if you will. This basket changes over time; in the past it's had cassette players, hot rotisserie cooked chicken and even face masks because that's what we were buying at the time. More recently, gluten free bread was included.

Fun fact: In 2024, vinyl records were added back in to the CPI basket of goods and services for the first time in 30 years, 'reflecting a resurgence in popularity'.

The prices are compared to what they were a year ago. So, when you hear inflation was 7 per cent last month, it means prices were, on average, 7 per cent higher than they were at the same time last year. This number is usually a bit old by the time you hear it; if we're in June, the inflation figures you see might be from May, which is why it's often called a backwards-looking metric. The BOE actually uses the CPI as its inflation metric.

Then there's CPIH, which is like CPI's slightly beefed-up sibling. It includes everything CPI does but also adds housing costs into the mix: things like rent, council tax and even the cost of owning a home. It gives a fuller picture of what's really going on with the cost of living, especially if you're a homeowner or renter.

Now, let's touch on RPI. RPI is another way of measuring inflation, but it's a bit different from CPI. It includes some things CPI doesn't, such as mortgage interest payments, which makes it particularly sensitive to changes in interest rates. However, it's not as commonly used these days because it's considered less accurate. But you might still hear about it in relation to things like train fare increases and student loans, or if you're looking at the interest on some government bonds.

Causes of inflation

Now, let's talk about why inflation happens, because it's not just some random occurrence. There are a few key drivers:

Demand-pull inflation: think of this as 'too much money chasing too few goods'. When there's a high demand for products or services but not enough supply, prices naturally go up. Imagine a hot new tech gadget everyone wants: stores can't keep it on the shelves, so the price shoots up.

Cost-push inflation occurs when the costs to produce goods go up, and businesses pass those costs on to consumers. For example, if the price of oil skyrockets, transporting goods becomes more expensive, and those costs are added to the price you pay at the checkout.

Sometimes, inflation becomes a self-fulfilling cycle. When workers expect prices to rise, they push for higher wages to keep up. Businesses, in turn, raise prices to cover these wage increases, leading to a cycle known as the wage-price spiral, where wages and prices keep driving each other up.

These inflation drivers affect almost everything we buy, and in recent years, they've contributed to what's often called the cost-of-living crisis. As prices rise faster than wages, purchasing power declines, meaning our money doesn't stretch as far as it used to. While we're still paying the same taxes, we're able to buy less with the same paycheque.

Inflation doesn't just impact what we buy; it also affects our savings and investments. When inflation rises faster than the interest rates on savings, the real value of money in the bank decreases over time. Understanding these concepts is crucial for managing finances effectively and protecting our purchasing power and savings in an inflationary environment.

How does this impact me?

While the ONS might report that inflation is, say, 2 per cent year-on-year, that number is really just an average. For you personally, inflation might feel more like 5 per cent or maybe even just 1 per cent, depending on your individual buying habits. The statistics represent price changes for the 'average' person, but here's the thing: you're not average, and neither are your spending habits.

The goods and services used to track inflation are chosen to represent the typical spending habits of the population. But how closely do your habits match the average person? If you're someone who shops at M&S, travels frequently or enjoys dining out, inflation might hit your budget harder. On the other hand, if you're cycling to work, cooking in bulk with a slow cooker, and avoiding splurges, your personal inflation rate might feel much lower.

Inflation, in reality, is personal. The prices that rise or don't rise are going to affect each of us differently based on where and how we spend our money. So, while the headline inflation number is useful as a general indicator, it's important to understand how your unique lifestyle and spending habits shape your own experience of inflation. That's why it can feel so different from person to person.

What can I do about it?

The first step in tackling inflation is understanding it. Knowing how inflation works and how it impacts different areas of your life can empower you to make informed decisions to protect your finances.

Take broadband as an example. Broadband services are part of the CPI inflation 'basket', and providers are often allowed to increase fees each year, sometimes even above the general rate of inflation. So, while inflation might be reported at 3 per cent, your broadband bill could go up by 6 per cent or more. Since these price hikes also push inflation higher overall, it becomes a bit of a vicious cycle. There are campaigns to cap these increases, but in the meantime, you can take control by:

- Shopping around for competitive rates to see if another provider offers a better deal.
- Locking in a fixed-rate contract to avoid unexpected price hikes.
- Reducing services you don't need to streamline your bill.

Adjust your budget

Inflation means some expenses are likely to rise more than others, so keeping a close eye on your spending and adjusting where possible can make a big difference.

Identify the areas of your budget that inflation hits the hardest, such as groceries, fuel and utilities. Consider:

- Setting spending limits for each category and monitoring them closely to avoid overspending.
- Prioritising essential expenses while trimming discretionary spending.
- Tracking price changes for regular purchases like groceries, and see if there's room to cut back or switch to more affordable options.

By understanding where inflation impacts your wallet the most, and by adjusting your budget and spending habits accordingly, you can minimise its effects on your financial health. Proactive planning and smarter spending will help you stretch your money further, ensuring you can navigate these challenging times with greater financial stability.

THINGS YOU NEED TO REMEMBER:

- While the official inflation rate is based on a general 'basket' of goods, your personal inflation rate depends on your own spending habits. Understanding your unique expenses can help you adjust more effectively.

- Inflation occurs due to factors like high demand, increased production costs and wage-price spirals.

- Tactics like shopping around for competitive rates, adjusting your budget for essentials, and taking advantage of loyalty programmes can help reduce inflation's effect on your finances.

PART THREE
Your Money

Your money might come from various places, but for most people, it starts with their monthly payslip from their employer. While it might seem like just a record of what you've earned, your payslip is an essential document, and knowing how to read it can make a huge difference in managing your money. This chapter will break down everything you need to know to understand, verify and take control of what's coming in. After all, it's your responsibility to make sure that your pay is accurate and that all your information is correct.

But what if your income doesn't only come from your job? If you're someone who earns money outside of their salary, we'll cover everything 'extra'. Whether you're self-employed, renting out a room in your home, or have a thriving side hustle, like selling clothes on Vinted, you'll learn how to handle and manage all those 'other' income streams, too.

In short, this is *your* money, and you're firmly in the driver's seat.

Think back to when you received your first payslip. You'd just finished your first month of work, excited to see that hard-earned money land in your account. Then you opened the payslip, and there it was, an array of unfamiliar terms like 'gross pay', 'net pay' and 'national insurance', plus deductions that seemed to chip away at the number you were expecting. It's easy to feel lost with all the jargon, wondering if you're missing out on income or if you fully understand what's happening with your pay.

If you've ever felt that initial confusion, you're not alone. As we dive into these chapters, we'll clarify what each line of your payslip means and explore other income streams, so you can confidently take charge of *your money.*

6. Understanding Your Payslip

Every month, when you get paid, you receive a payslip, whether in paper form or, more commonly now, online. This document breaks down your earnings, including how much goes to national insurance, tax, pension contributions and, if applicable, student loan repayments.

Your payslip is your responsibility. Mistakes can happen, and you need to know what 'right' looks like so that you can spot any discrepancies when something's wrong.

When I first started working, I assumed I'd missed a lesson somewhere, a session where someone, perhaps a Yoda-type colleague full of wisdom, would walk me through my payslip and explain each section wearing traditional Jedi robes. Turns out, nobody's assigned to teach you this. Maybe you were fortunate enough to have a parent who showed you how their payslips worked, but even then, they may have looked different from yours.

While your payroll or HR team is responsible for processing your pay correctly, that doesn't guarantee it'll always be right. They often use automated systems, but errors can still occur. This is where you come in: taking control by double-checking each month ensures you're being paid correctly and helps you build confidence in understanding your income.

You may find that your payslip looks accurate month after month, and the process of checking it seems tedious. But consider this: mistakes tend to pop up when you least expect them. Keeping an eye on your payslip might seem like a small task, but it's essential for financial control.

Understanding your payslip gives you valuable insights into how taxes and deductions work, where your money goes before it reaches your bank account, and any hidden benefits, like pensions or employee perks. Your payslip is like a map, guiding you to a clear picture of your take-home pay and how it's calculated. Skipping over it means missing out on the foundation of financial literacy. Knowing how to interpret your payslip empowers you to negotiate better, budget smarter, and avoid unpleasant surprises like unexpected tax adjustments.

So let's tackle this together and turn 'future you's problem' into something you're equipped to manage with confidence.

How to read your payslip

We will start from the top of your payslip and work our way through it (there is an example of a payslip below), but most payslips work the same way.

Company:	Name:	Date: 30/04/2025	NI Number: JZ 25 91 87 C

Earnings:		Deductions:	
Salary	£2,500.00	Income Tax	£270.70
Overtime/Bonus	£0.00	EE National Insurance	£116.20
Pen Sacrifice 5%	-£99.00	Student Loan Plan 2	£20.00
Total	£2,401.00	Total	£406.90

Elent Ltd

Tax Month: 1	Employee Number: 1234ABC	Year To Date:	
		Total Gross Pay TD	£2,500.00
		Tax TD	£270.70
Tax Code: 1257L	Department: Finance	EE NI TD	£116.20
		Student Loan TD	£20.00

PAYE ref: 1234/XYZ/12	Payment Method: BACS	Payment Period: Monthly	Net Pay: £1,994.10

The 'admin' details

First off, at the top of your payslip, you should see your company name and your name, followed by the date the payslip was issued. The company name might be different from the one you're actually working for if they have a parent company, but your name should always be in full on your payslip.

You should also see your address; it is important that this is up to date. If you move, it is one of the essential parts of admin you need to do because while yes, payslips are often distributed digitally, you may still receive letters around changes to tax codes, for instance, which you will miss if your address is wrong on your company's payroll system.

95

The date is the date you are paid, and for many of you who've never received a payslip before, this happens in the last week of the month. Very rarely, a company might do this mid-month – in any case, your fellow colleagues will be able to tell you when payday is; they might not remember what pension provider you're with, but everyone – I mean everyone – knows when payday is.

Next up is your national insurance number, which is the nine-character individual reference code given to you between your 15th and 16th birthday. Think of it as a less exciting version of your Hogwarts letter. This lets HMRC track your national insurance contributions, and we'll look at this in detail on page 249.

Good to know: If you don't know where your insurance number is, or you want to check that your national insurance number is correct on your payslip, you can download the HMRC app. This will give you the ability to actually put your national insurance number into your phone wallet, just like you put your bank cards in there, which is very helpful.

The earnings box

Now, we are on to the earnings box, sometimes called payments or income. Let's start with your basic pay or gross salary. The gross salary is where your income starts; this is your annual salary divided by 12 on a monthly payslip.

As well as your basic salary, which is fixed and regular, you may have bonuses and commissions; what are they?

In certain careers, bonuses and commissions are a significant part of an employee's total earnings. These additional payments can be seen as rewards for exceptional performance, achieving specific targets or contributing to the success of a project. However, understanding how these bonuses and commissions appear on your payslip and how they are taxed is crucial for effectively understanding the rest of the tax and take-home pay.

Bonuses are typically one-time payments given to employees as a reward for meeting certain performance criteria. These can be annual bonuses based on overall company performance, quarterly bonuses tied to specific goals, or even spot bonuses for extraordinary achievements.

Commissions, on the other hand, are variable payments based on the level of sales or business generated by an employee. Common in sales roles, commissions provide an incentive for employees to increase their productivity and contribute directly to the company's revenue.

Imagine you work for a company that sells top-of-the-line espresso machines. You're on a base salary, but the real money is in commissions: every time you sell a machine, you earn a little extra on top of your regular pay. Now, you've got a coworker named Sam who's a legend in the office for his sales skills. Sam doesn't just stop at hitting his target; he's often surpassing it and raking in serious commission.

Last month, for instance, Sam set a personal record by selling 30 machines in just a few weeks. Every sale earned him a 5 per cent commission, meaning that for each £2,000 espresso machine he sold, he pocketed an extra £100. By the end of the month, Sam had added £3,000 in commissions to his base pay, all from selling the machines he was already hired to promote. Not only did Sam bring in a nice bonus, but he also boosted the company's revenue, which is exactly what commissions are designed to do.

So, in a role like Sam's, commissions don't just reward you for a job well done, they motivate you to aim higher, because the more machines you sell, the bigger your payout. And that's how companies use commissions as a way to inspire productivity and reward employees for directly contributing to the bottom line.

This separation helps both you and HMRC understand the make-up of your total income. One other line of income you might see in your earnings box could be overtime for extra hours worked beyond your basic pay. These income streams all come together to be counted as one amount.

Pension contributions

We've wrapped up the income you get in, but there's something else you might see in your earnings box:

pension contributions. They are an integral part of your payslip and one aspect of it that you do have control over. How much you choose to contribute, how much your employer contributes, or even if you choose to contribute at all are all decisions made by you, and they can change from month to month.

Most employees are automatically enrolled in a workplace pension if they meet certain criteria. This auto-enrolment scheme was introduced to encourage everyone to save for their future, but participation isn't mandatory. If you're enrolled, you can choose to opt-out, and after three years, you'll be re-enrolled with the option to opt-out again if desired.

Currently, about 90 per cent of employees contribute to workplace pensions, which is a positive trend for future financial security. While auto-enrolment is the standard route for many, it's not the only way to save for retirement. You can find other strategies in the pensions chapter.

Interestingly, there's also ongoing discussion about a 'pot for life' pension model similar to Australia's superannuation system. In Australia, there's a unified pension pot that follows individuals throughout their careers, with contributions based on returns from investments rather than a guaranteed minimum income. We'll dive deeper into the pros and cons of these different pension models in Chapter 14.

On your payslip, pension contributions are often labelled as 'pen sacrifice', 'pension' or 'auto-enrolment', all of which refer to your workplace pension contributions. Typically, 5 per cent of your income is automatically deducted as a minimum contribution, with your employer adding another 3 per cent, bringing the total to 8 per cent.

However, many companies offer enhanced contributions. For example, let's consider someone named Alex. Alex's employer offers a matching contribution of up to 8 per cent. Alex previously contributed the standard 5 per cent, with their employer contributing 3 per cent. However, by increasing their own contribution to 8 per cent, Alex was able to get their employer to match it, doubling the contribution amount to 16 per cent each month. In just one adjustment, Alex's savings grew significantly, thanks to the employer match.

So why would someone like Alex choose to contribute more? The answer often comes down to tax benefits. Pension contributions in the UK come with tax relief, which means the government essentially adds to your contributions by refunding some of the tax you've already paid. For most taxpayers, this starts at the basic rate of 20 per cent. For example, if you contribute £80 into your pension, the government adds another £20, making it a total of £100 in your pension pot.

If you're a higher-rate (40 per cent) taxpayer, you can claim an additional 20 per cent tax relief (to match your tax band), and if you're an additional-rate (45 per cent) taxpayer, you can claim an additional 25 per cent. This additional tax relief doesn't automatically go into your pension but must be claimed through a self-assessment tax return. By doing this, you reduce the total amount of tax you pay on your income, making pension contributions a highly tax-efficient way to save for the future.

The deductions, whether 5 per cent, 8 per cent or more, are taken from your gross income, which reduces your taxable income accordingly. By understanding and adjusting your contributions, you're making decisions today that will benefit your future financial well-being.

Deductions

Now that we've covered income, let's break down the deductions section. Deductions determine your take-home pay by showing the amounts that are subtracted from your gross income.

First, let's define *taxable income*: it's what's left after everything in the earnings box is accounted for, your gross income plus any bonuses or commissions minus pension contributions. The lower your taxable income, the less tax you'll pay, so pension contributions and other adjustments can make a significant difference.

The deductions box on your payslip will show the main types of taxes and contributions taken out each month, including income tax and national insurance.

Income tax is done on a threshold basis, so on income between £0 and £12,570 (as of writing this), you pay zero tax. This is called your personal allowance, and we're going to dive into this a bit more when we talk about tax codes.

After that, you pay a basic rate of 20 per cent between £12,570 and £50,270, followed by the higher rate of 40 per cent, which is chargeable between £50,270 and £125,140. And finally, the additional rate is 45 per cent, and that is anything over £125,140.

However, if you're earning over £100,000 a year, a hidden complication can arise known as the 60 per cent tax trap. Here's how it works: when your income exceeds £100,000, you start to lose your tax-free personal allowance by £1 for every £2 earned above this threshold. For the income between £100,000 and £125,140, this effectively adds up to a marginal tax rate of 60 per cent, meaning you're both paying the higher rate of 40 per cent and losing your personal allowance.

In no other tax system would this be acceptable, but because it doesn't impact the majority of people, it's rarely discussed. And due to fiscal drag – a phenomenon where tax thresholds don't keep pace with inflation or wage growth – people are gradually pulled into higher tax brackets over time. This means that though your income may not feel significantly higher, you end up paying more tax because the thresholds haven't increased in line with rising earnings.

For someone like Alex, who has the average UK salary of around £36,700, their income tax would be calculated as follows:

- The first £12,570 is tax-free.
- On the remaining £24,130 (from £12,570 to £36,700), they pay the basic rate of 20 per cent.

This means Alex will pay around £4,824 annually in income tax, or approximately £402 per month. Knowing these thresholds helps Alex understand why their taxable income might fluctuate and how any additional income (like a bonus) would be taxed.

The second of the employment taxes in your deductions box is national insurance. Sometimes, on payslips, you might see income tax and national insurance wrapped up together, sometimes just called 'tax' or 'PAYE', but they are definitely two separate taxes.

National insurance rates are calculated based on income thresholds. For example, similar to income tax, you pay zero tax on earnings up to £12,570. The basic rate is currently set at 8 per cent. In 2023, under Rishi Sunak's government, this basic rate was reduced from 12 per cent to 10 per cent and then further down to 8 per cent. For higher earners, there is a flat rate of 2 per cent.

Since Alex earns £36,700, their national insurance is calculated on income above £12,570. This means paying 8 per cent on the remaining £24,130, resulting in an annual NI contribution of around £1,930, or about £160 per month.

In years gone by, national insurance contributions used to go into the national insurance fund, which finances the state pension for today's retirees, as well as funding the NHS and other essential services we often take for granted. There is no 'separate' pot anymore. It is one central pot, and all aspects of the state are funded from income tax, NI, VAT and other pots.

Something else to note about NI is who pays it; yes, we know it comes out of our payslip in the deduction box. That is called employee national insurance. But your employer also pays NI – on your behalf – cleverly named employer national insurance.

Let's put this all together with Alex's payslip. Alex's gross salary of £36,700 is subject to both income tax and NI. Here's a simplified breakdown:

- **Income Tax**: £4,824 annually or about £402 monthly.
- **National Insurance**: £1,930 annually or about £160 monthly.

This brings Alex's total deductions to around £562 per month. This means Alex's take-home pay, after these deductions, is approximately £2,495 each month.

Additionally, Alex has chosen to contribute the standard 5 per cent to their pension. This contribution means Alex's employer will also be contributing, adding up to a total pension contribution of 8 per cent (5 per cent from Alex and 3 per cent from the employer). This not only reduces Alex's taxable income but also boosts retirement savings significantly.

Why do we pay two different taxes?

Great question. The two taxes are likely to be merged in the future for administrative reasons, but one of the current reasons why it is split out is for the state pension. The NI contributions you make show HMRC your eligibility for the state pension. To qualify for the full state pension, you have to pay NI contributions or get them in some capacity for at least 10 years, and 35 years to receive the full amount.

Other deductions you might see

We knew taxes were coming, right? But what we might not know about are the other deductions available to us. Many businesses will offer other tax relief in the form of salary sacrifices; not every business will offer everything below, but I've listed all of them just to show you what could be available.

- Salary sacrifice schemes: there are many different types of these, such as cycle-to-work schemes – paying for a bike upfront and seeing the monthly payments come out of your salary.
- Union or professional membership fees – as an accountant, I pay a membership fee each year, and for many other industries like teaching and lawyers, these fees can be quite steep. Paying them off monthly through your employer will be shown on your payslip.

- Private healthcare, which can include full coverage or cash services where you get a discount on dentistry.
- Gym memberships can also be put through your business, which you pay off through your salary.
- Travel season passes – purchasing an annual train ticket often saves you a lot of money but comes with a hefty upfront cost, and many companies will let you pay for it through them and then have the cost deducted from your payslip each month.
- Give as you earn – charity donations.

It is worth reviewing which benefits your employer offers because some of these mean tax relief at source, saving you money with very little effort on your part.

The final deduction we can see here is student loans (and we'll explore these more in Chapter 10).

You will only see a student loan deduction when you have left university and are starting to pay back the loan you borrowed. It is automatically taken from your payslip for many reasons, but the main one is ease for the Student Loans Company.

To work out how much you are paying back on your payslip, take your gross pay, which is your annual basic salary but also includes any bonuses and commissions you've received in the month. If you think of it on an annual basis, take the monthly income you're getting and multiply it by 12 to work out your annual income. Then deduct the threshold for your student loan plan. (Which student loan plan you're on depends on which year you went to university. See page 190.) Then, similar to a tax, you pay 9 per cent of your total salary above the threshold. Divide that figure by 12 to find out how much you're paying each month.

When you start a new job, your employer will need to know if you went to university and did any form of qualification, undergraduate or postgraduate and took out a student loan to go with it. The payroll team take it from there, where they'll choose the plan you were on, and the deductions will come out of your payslip automatically.

Elent Ltd	
Tax Month:	Employee Number:
1	1234ABC
Tax Code:	Department:
1257L	Finance

Tax codes

Tax codes might look like just another set of letters and numbers on your payslip, but they're one of the most important details when it comes to how much tax you're paying, as they tell HMRC how much of your income is tax-free each year. So it's vital to understand what your code means and how it affects your take-home pay.

The numbers in your tax code represent your personal allowance. For example, the code 1257L – the most common tax code – means you can earn £12,570 before income tax kicks in.

If your tax code is 1250L, this means you have a slightly lower personal allowance (£12,500) for some reason. Maybe you've claimed tax-deductible expenses, or HMRC is recouping underpaid tax from previous years.

If you see 0T, that means you've used up your personal allowance or don't have one, and you'll pay tax on all your income.

The letters in your tax code give HMRC extra information about your tax situation. Here are some common ones:

L – Standard tax code for people entitled to the basic personal allowance.

T – Emergency tax code, used when HMRC doesn't have full information about your income (such as when you change jobs). It means you might pay too much or too little tax until it's corrected. It can also be due to adjustments on your tax code.

S – For residents of Scotland who have different income tax bands.

C – For residents of Wales, reflecting Welsh income tax rates.

M1 – (month 1) – A 'non-cumulative' tax code, meaning tax is calculated on a monthly basis rather than taking into account what you've already earned this year. It's often used when you start a new job.

D0 – Income taxed at the 40% tax rate
D1 – Income taxed at the 45% tax rate

Marriage Allowance

Marriage Allowance is a tax break for married couples or civil partners, allowing one partner to transfer up to 10 per cent of their personal allowance to the other. It's particularly useful if one partner earns less than the personal allowance threshold.

- N – If you transfer 10 per cent of your personal allowance to your spouse.
- M – If your spouse has transferred 10 per cent of their allowance to you.

For example, if your partner doesn't earn enough to use their full personal allowance, they can transfer a portion of it to you. This can reduce your tax bill and leave you with more money in your pocket.

What happens when I get a tax code change? Should I inform my employer?

When your tax code changes, HMRC will contact your employer as well as you to explain that your tax code has been changed with details as to why. If you notice after a month or two that you're not seeing a tax code change it's worth chatting to your payroll team just in case the letter has been misplaced; they definitely should have received one.

Why might my tax code change?

Underpaid or overpaid tax: If you've underpaid or overpaid tax in previous years, HMRC might adjust your tax code to either collect what you owe or give you a refund.

Marriage allowance: If you've transferred or received part of a spouse's allowance, your tax code will reflect this.

Savings or other income: If you have additional income from savings or investments, HMRC can adjust your tax code to account for the tax owed on this extra income.

What if my tax code is wrong?

1. Check the HMRC app. It's a great tool to see your tax code and find out exactly how it's been calculated.
2. If something still seems off, contact HMRC directly. They'll be able to explain why your tax code is what it is and make corrections if necessary.
3. If HMRC confirms they've sent the right information to your employer and you're not seeing it reflected, speak to your payroll or HR team.

The tax year

In the UK, the tax year doesn't align with the calendar year; it runs from 6 April to 5 April the following year. What this means is that your payslip won't show 'year-to-date' summaries based on the calendar year but rather on the tax year.

This number becomes important when you're looking at your tax deductions or any year-to-date summaries. Everything you see on your payslip relates to the tax year rather than the calendar year. So when you're reviewing your payslip, and it shows 'total tax paid to date' or 'total national insurance to date,' it's showing the amount you've paid since 6 April, not since 1 January.

For example, if it's June, and you've paid £1,200 in income tax, that total is calculated based on your earnings and tax deductions from the start of the tax year in April. This is something to keep in mind when you're checking your payslip, particularly if you're used to thinking in calendar years.

History fact: When we used the Julian calendar, our calendar year started at the beginning of spring, hence April. In 1752, we moved from the Julian calendar to the Gregorian calendar, and effectively 'lost' 11 days to synchronise with Europe. The accountants just couldn't cope with the change, so we kept the tax year running from April to April. Who knows, maybe it was because accountants just didn't want to finish a fiscal year in the depth of winter or interrupt singing 'Auld Lang Syne'.

Employee number

This is not to be confused with your national insurance number; it is given to you by your employer. If you work in a small business, you might not have an employee number, but in many large organisations, it's a simple way to keep track of you. When you leave your job, your employee number doesn't follow you.

Department

When I use this payslip example in schools, I often say I am not being very creative and just list everyone as working in finance, and I'll say the same to you. This is your book; take that biro and go wild, cross it out and write the department you work in or the pipe-dream job. You're likely to see a department on your payslip, and if you don't, this is also fine. It's a signpost for the HR and payroll team rather than something that has an impact on your income.

TD – to date
EE NI – employee national insurance
Year to date – tax year-to-date

Year To Date:

Total Gross Pay TD	£2,500.00
Tax TD	£270.70
EE NI TD	£116.20
Student Loan TD	£20.00

Another way you can see this summary is through a P60; this form outlines your yearly earnings. Think of it like a yearly payslip, just outlining everything that happened in the year financially from you to HMRC.

Two other forms to be aware of with regard to pay are:

- P45 – the big bad wolf of the employment forms; this is the document you're either handed when you're asked to leave or the one you get when you walk away of your own accord. Either way, you're getting this, and your employer hands it to HMRC to inform them that you've ceased working for the company.
- P11D – A form your employer gives HMRC that tells them any employee benefits you receive, such as a company car or medical insurance.

Final elements

PAYE reference code: the Pay As You Earn system by which your employer pays your taxes on your behalf uses a reference code to make sure your income tax and national insurance tax are paid.

Payment method: BACS stands for bank automated clearing system; your employer pays your income directly from their bank account to yours; very rarely is anyone paid in cash now, but the payslip will illustrate this.

Take-home pay

This is where we end on the payslip, and it's the good bit: net pay. This is your take-home wage: £1,994.10 from a £30k annual salary. That is what hits your bank account and what you can spend. We've been through the wild ride of the payslip, from gross to net pay, we've lost money to our future self in the way of pensions, we've paid money into the system in the form of taxes and also paid some of our student loans back.

What happens when you have a pay rise?

Getting a pay rise is always exciting, but it's important to understand how that extra cash affects the rest of your finances, from taxes to student loans. The key thing to remember is that with a pay rise, it's not just your take-home pay that changes; your tax liability, national insurance and possibly other deductions will be affected, too.

Say you've had a pay rise that keeps you within the basic-rate tax band. For example, if your salary jumps from £20k to £25k, you'll see an increase in your gross pay, which will result in a higher income tax liability and potentially larger student loan deductions.

Student loans: If you're on Plan 1, which applies to people who started university before 2012, you'll begin to see larger deductions from your payslip, as Plan 1 kicks in once you earn over £22,015. And for those on Plan 2 or later, which applies to students who started university after 2012, you won't start repaying until your salary hits £27,295. So, if your salary is still under this threshold, your student loan deductions won't increase yet.

Now, let's say your salary increases from £50k to £55k. This bump will push you into the higher-rate tax band, and here's what that means:

Higher income tax: You'll pay 40 per cent tax on income that exceeds £50,270. While your personal allowance (the first £12,570) remains tax-free, everything above the basic rate band will be taxed at 40 per cent.

Student loan deductions: Your student loan repayments will also increase since they're calculated as a percentage of your income above the repayment threshold.

But there's more to consider. Moving into a higher salary band affects other areas of your finances:

Savings and dividends impact

Personal savings allowance: If you are a higher rate tax payer, your personal savings allowance (the amount of interest you can earn on savings without being taxed) drops from £1,000 to £500. Any interest you earn over that allowance will be taxed at a higher rate (40 per cent). If you are an additional-rate taxpayer, you do not have a personal savings allowance.

Dividends: If you receive dividend income, the first £500 is tax-free, but any dividend income above that is taxed at 33.75 per cent instead of the 8.75 per cent rate applied to basic-rate taxpayers. So, be prepared to pay more tax if you're receiving dividends from investments or shares.

Do I have to pay tax on my bonus?

Yes, bonuses are taxed just like regular salary, potentially pushing you into a higher tax bracket and increasing deductions like national insurance and student loan payments. With some planning, however, you can soften the tax impact. If you're receiving a large bonus, think about using salary sacrifice by directing a portion into your pension; this will reduce your taxable income and build up your pension pot. Contributions to your pension not only shelter that amount from immediate tax but can even bring your effective income below higher tax thresholds, making a substantial difference in what you keep.

For example, let's say you receive a £5,000 bonus on top of your £45k salary, bringing your total annual income to £50k. This would move you closer to the higher tax rate threshold. Unfortunately, even bonuses are subject to the same tax rates and deductions as your regular salary, so a bonus is never tax-free. If you're still repaying a student loan, your repayments will increase based on the bonus amount as well.

Timing a promotion and reviewing your other income sources is a good idea; if you are earning near £100k and receiving childcare vouchers, you might find a pay rise to £105k is somewhat like a cliff edge where you no longer receive that benefit and may cost you money in the long run.

THINGS YOU NEED TO REMEMBER:

- Regularly review your payslip for accuracy, especially your pay and deductions.

- Ensure your tax code is correct, as it affects how much tax you pay.

- Know what's being deducted, like student loans and pensions, and how it impacts your pay.

7. Exploring Other Income Streams – money outside of your 9-5

In the previous chapter, we focused on understanding the income you receive from traditional employment. But in today's economy, for many, relying on a single paycheque isn't the full picture. Income can come from a variety of sources, whether it's a side hustle, selling clothes online, freelancing or being fully self-employed

This chapter is all about expanding your perspective on where your money can come from and how to make the most of multiple income streams. We'll dive into options that could boost your earnings and help build more financial freedom, whether you're looking to supplement your current job or consider full-time self-employment.

However, before starting, it's crucial to review your existing employment contract for any non-compete clauses. These clauses may restrict certain types of side work or freelance opportunities, so it's important to be aware of your employer's policies to avoid potential conflicts.

What is considered 'other money'?

When it comes to income, we first think about salary, but there are tons of other ways to make money that don't include an employer, a desk and a 9–5 schedule.

The standard rule for knowing when this other money is taxable is adhering to the trading allowance, often referred to as a side-hustle allowance, which is £1,000. This means if you earn £1k or less in the tax year outside of employment income, you don't have to declare it to HMRC.

HMRC established this allowance because they worked out that it would cost them more to organise the tax on this little revenue than it would to just let it go.

The list below – which is not comprehensive – suggests a few ways that you could be making money and what the obligations are from a financial perspective.

1. Your Home

For many people, a home is not just a place to live, but also a valuable asset that can be leveraged to generate extra income. One of the most straightforward ways to earn money from your home is by renting out a spare room. The Rent a Room Scheme is designed to encourage homeowners to let out furnished rooms in their homes to lodgers.

With this, you can earn up to £7,500 a year tax-free, but there are a few things to be aware of. If you go over this amount, there are tax liabilities, and you must be living in the house at the time.

If you are not renting a room, there are other ways to make money from your home, such as sites like Airbnb/Booking.com, which allow you to rent out your property or spare room to a guest. This falls into that £1k trading allowance we spoke about earlier. I do this myself once a year. I live quite close to Wimbledon tennis club, and for two weeks a year during the tennis championships, I go on holiday and rent my flat out. This could make sense to you if you're in a similar position where your flat or home is near an event. You have all the flexibility to choose your dates, and you can even choose the types of guests, such as specifying that you will only rent to those who have used the sites before and have good reviews. Just be careful and aware of the fees, as sometimes they can wipe out your profit and make it not really worth it.

2. Selling
In a society where online retailers can be shipping over 1 million pieces of clothing a month, no wonder we end up with things in our homes we don't really need but seemed like such a good deal when we bought them. This has led to the rise in sites like Vinted, which lets you sell your clothes for free, much like eBay.

Selling your clothes can be a quick way to make money. However, there are some tax implications if it becomes a business, so let me break it down.

If you are selling personal items, and the money you make over a tax year is less than what you paid for them, there is no tax payable. In the UK, platforms like Vinted and Depop are required to provide sellers information back to HMRC. Typically, if you sell items over approximately £1,700 or sell over 30 items, you will need to complete a seller report that will be sent back to HMRC, though again, if there is no profit and you are selling personal items, there is likely to be no tax due. If however, you are trading and operating for profit, this becomes taxable.

3. Freelance

Other low-cost options for additional income could be freelancing, using a skill you already have; this can take many forms, such as tutoring students in subjects you are great in. Performing a part-time role for another business and even public speaking could be considered freelance for many if it's ad hoc and happening outside your job.

It is worth reviewing your employment contracts when you start freelancing, as some contracts will forbid you from working for others or for yourself while working for them. It could create a conflict of interest.

There are also tax implications of working freelance; you will have to register as self-employed through the gov.uk website and file a self-assessment each year for the previous tax year.

4. Online

Influencers, content creators and YouTubers: there are numerous names now for the newest jobs in the market. There are opportunities for individuals to earn money through their creative outlets online. One of the most popular avenues is becoming an influencer or content creator. Building a personal brand on social media platforms such as Instagram, TikTok and YouTube and creating engaging content that attracts a large following means these creators can charge brands to promote their products or collaborate on ideas. The key to success in the online space lies in authenticity, creativity, consistency and the ability to engage with your audience meaningfully.

Affiliate marketing is closely related to this. Here, you can use your platforms to share product reviews, recommendations and links where you make a small percentage of sales made through your links. Success in affiliate marketing requires selecting the right products to promote and understanding your audience's needs. There are countless affiliate programmes available – Amazon and LTK are two of the big ones – and there's potential to earn a substantial income.

None of these jobs are tax free; all of your income is subject to income tax and national insurance when you earn enough.

When does other money become a business?

But when does all of this extra income stop being a 'side hustle' or just 'pocket money' and become a business that has its own tax liabilities and systems? This involves you being aware of how much you're making within the tax year – which runs from 6 April to 5 April.

What to be aware of:

The frequency of transactions and intention.

- How often are you renting out your room on Airbnb? Are you doing it for the odd week a year when you're also away, or are you, in fact, not living there, and this is a rental property?
- How often are you selling clothes through Depop or Vinted? Is it once a month or a quarter, having a clear-out and selling off last season's jeans that have magically sewn themselves tighter? Or are you buying clothes with no intention of wearing them but knowing you could sell them for more? Is it becoming a full-time commitment rather than a hobby?

The frequency may be easier to spot than the intention, but both matter. Did you intend to start selling five or more of the same product? Did it happen to be a busy rental month on Airbnb? The rest of the year is quiet. The two can be reviewed on a case-by-case basis, but keep a close eye. And neither one is the 'more important', but you would need to prove across both that it wasn't trading income.

If you are over these thresholds and realise that you are in fact trading, what then?

Well, you have a few options: one is to set yourself up as self-employed, and the second is to set up a business.

Self-employed

Being self-employed offers a range of freedoms and responsibilities that differ significantly from traditional employment. You can also be both self-employed and employed; if there is income outside of your employed income that needs to be declared, that is your responsibility.

To start the process, you must register for self-assessment; it's the process in which you report your income to HMRC. You are responsible for your own report and paying the tax, which is, of course, different from the payslip we covered in Chapter 6, which is organised by your employer.

You might also find yourself filling in a self-assessment as a higher or additional earner already, and this might be to gain back your tax relief on your pensions which we spoke about before and/or possibly if there are repayments to be paid in the case of childcare allowance.

Registering as self-employed must be done by 5 October following the end of the tax year in which you became self-employed – i.e. when you started trading above the allowances you're given.

One frustrating element that catches people out is something called 'payment on accounts'; this is where HMRC requires advance payments towards your tax bill. These payments on account are due on 31 January and 31 July each year and are based on your previous year's tax bill. This system ensures that your tax payments are spread throughout the year, reducing the burden of a large single payment.

A word of warning: If you are at any point worried that you might miss a deadline or you've received a letter saying you need to fill in a self-assessment, but you don't think you do, DO NOT ignore it. It can lead to fines and future frustrations. Contact HMRC and explain your case to avoid those penalties and interest charges.

Being a business

One of the easiest ways to differentiate between operating as a business and as a sole trader individual is the formation of a limited company. It costs just £12 to set up a limited company on the gov.uk website, which is why more than 500,000 are established on average every year.

One of the key benefits of forming a limited company is limited liability. This means that the personal assets of the shareholders are protected in the event that the company faces financial difficulties. The shareholders' liability is limited to the amount they have invested in the company.

Operating as a limited company can enhance a business's credibility and professionalism. It often makes it easier to attract investment, secure loans and build trust with clients and suppliers.

A significant historical moment in the UK's corporate landscape occurred when then-chancellor Gordon

Brown introduced a zero rate of tax for businesses earning below a certain threshold. This policy led to a surge in the formation of limited companies, nearly crashing the government website as entrepreneurs rushed to take advantage.

A limited company, whether labelled Limited, Ltd, or another variation, is a separate legal entity. This distinction means that for HMRC purposes, it stands alone, independent from its owners. It has its own tax system, separate from personal income tax, and requires its own bookkeeping and financial records.

As a limited company, you're a corporate entity, separate from the person who pays corporation tax and can take the income out as a dividend, which incurs its own dividend tax but not national insurance, or you could even take it out as capital gains if the company wraps up.

There are more taxes involved, but the rates might be lower, and as a business, there are far more expenses you can offset against your revenue to reduce your taxable profit than if you're a sole trader.

Paying yourself when you're a sole trader means when income comes in you pay taxes such as income and national insurance tax on that income annually, much like you see on your payslip. It is just done through the self-assessment online system, and you can reduce the income you pay tax on by using the trading allowance of £1k or putting your expenses through to reduce the revenue or increase pension contributions. That is it.

However, as a business owner, deciding how to pay

yourself involves tax planning – paying yourself while reducing your tax liability. There can be costs you can deduct in a business that you can't do if you are a sole trader.

Taking income as a salary, you, as the business owner, can pay yourself as director whichever income you choose. Some people choose to pay themselves £12,570 a year; keeping their income below the NI and Income tax thresholds means at year-end, there won't be any tax to pay.

You can also withdraw money in other ways, such as through dividends. We will see this word come up again in Part 5 around building wealth as dividends can come out of investing in the stock market, but for this purpose, let me explain.

Dividends

Dividends are payments made to shareholders from the company's profits after corporation tax. As a business owner, you can take dividends in addition to your salary. You are a shareholder as a director and can therefore dictate (to a certain extent) the dividends you want to pay out.

There is a dividend allowance, similar to other allowances like personal and national insurance and trading. This allowance is currently £500 a year, but it has dropped significantly in the last few years.

The reason people choose to pay themselves dividends

rather than an increased salary is the tax rates. As we have discussed, for income tax, the basic rate stands at 20, higher 40 and additional 45 per cent; however, for dividends, the rates are 8.75 per cent basic, 33.75 per cent higher and 39.35 per cent additional. All are slightly lower, reducing the tax paid on the revenue you take out. There is also no national insurance to be paid on dividend income.

This is not a guide to paying yourself a salary, but many people take a combination of dividends and salary, and being aware of what is on offer can reduce the tax you pay and make sure you have income when needed.

The finance bits of a business you need to know

If you've considered running a business or you are currently a business owner, you will find there are many financial reports that, on the outside, seem really confusing and overcomplicate matters. Sadly, they are requirements, but let's go through them together.

First is the famous profit and loss report (P&L), which sets out your revenue streams and lists your deductions.

Profits are determined by subtracting the company's expenses from its total revenue. These expenses can include salaries, rent and operational expenses.

The primary tax applicable to limited companies that isn't relevant to any other entities in the UK is corporation tax. This tax is levied on the profits made by the company.

As of 2024, the corporation tax rate in the UK is 25 per cent for companies with profits over £250,000 and 19 per cent for smaller companies with profits below £50,000. There is a sliding scale of rates between £50,000 and £250,000.

And if you think of a P&L as a yearly look at financials, the balance sheet is more like a 'snapshot' of a certain time; it shows what a company owns (its assets), what it owes (its liabilities) and the value left for the owners (equity) at a specific point in time. It is a snapshot that shows where the company stands financially, its resources, its debts and what's left after paying off the debts.

In the tax chapter, we touched on VAT, but there's more to it when you're running a business. If your business has an annual turnover above £90,000, you'll need to submit a VAT report on a quarterly basis. This report details both the VAT you've charged on your sales (income) and the VAT you've paid on your expenses. To calculate what you owe, you'll subtract the VAT on your expenses from the VAT on your sales. The remaining amount is your VAT liability, which is what you need to pay to HMRC.

Parental leave

Parental leave is a significant aspect of preparing for parenthood, especially when it comes to understanding your rights and what support is available to you as a working parent in the UK. It's crucial to navigate this period with a clear understanding of the financial implications and the time you'll have to spend with your new arrival. Here's what you need to know.

If you're an employee, you're entitled to up to 52 weeks of maternity leave, broken into ordinary maternity leave (26 weeks) and additional maternity leave (another 26 weeks). Statutory maternity pay (SMP) covers the first 39 weeks, with 90 per cent of your average weekly earnings for six weeks, then £184.03 (or 90 per cent of your weekly earnings, whichever is lower) for the next 33 weeks. SMP is subject to tax and national insurance, so be sure to budget for this income change.

Some employers go beyond the statutory minimum and offer enhanced maternity pay. This could mean full pay for a specified period or an increase in SMP rates. Often, this benefit is conditional on your returning to work for a certain period, usually between three and six months. If you leave before that time, a clawback policy might mean repaying some or all of the enhanced benefits. Always check these details before finalising your maternity leave plans.

The shared parental leave (SPL) scheme allows parents to share up to 50 weeks of leave and up to 37 weeks of pay, offering flexibility in caring for their child. You can alternate leave with your partner or take leave together, depending on what works best. To qualify for SPL, both partners must meet specific employment criteria. Adoption leave and pay are similar to maternity leave and can be shared through SPL as well.

During maternity leave, you're allowed up to ten keeping in touch (KIT) days. These can be used for work purposes like training or important meetings, allowing you to stay engaged without affecting your SMP. Employers usually pay KIT days at your usual day rate, but they're legally only required to pay the national minimum wage. Some may also deduct your KIT day payment from your SMP, so clarify this in advance.

On maternity leave, you continue to accrue annual leave and, if applicable, bank holidays. Legally, you cannot take holiday and maternity leave simultaneously, so any unused holiday can be taken when you return. If you're considering leaving your job, waiting until the end of your maternity leave to resign (keeping in mind your notice period) can help you accrue holiday entitlement, which may provide a small financial buffer.

For fathers, the situation is a bit different. Statutory paternity leave is currently set at just two weeks – sorry dads – which many feel is insufficient time to bond with a new child or support a partner during the crucial early days. This limited leave is one of the reasons why discussions about shared parental leave and extending paternity leave continue to be a significant topic in the workplace and beyond.

If you're self-employed, the situation changes again. While you're not eligible for statutory maternity pay, you can apply for maternity allowance. This allowance is typically lower than the SMP available to employees, offering a maximum of £172.48 per week for up to 39 weeks. This can be a financial challenge, so it's crucial to plan and budget for this period well in advance.

In conclusion, navigating parental leave requires understanding your rights and the benefits available to you, whether you're an employee or self-employed. It's important to take advantage of the support provided, know your entitlements, and prepare financially for this important time in your life. With the right information, you can focus on what matters most: spending precious time with your new family member.

Child benefit

This is a benefit given out by the government for having children between birth and up to 16 or 20 if they're in full-time education or training. There is a set amount given for your first child and then every subsequent child after that. There are rules for any benefit, and there are still billions of pounds in untapped benefit money that people don't realise they're eligible for, and therefore, it's left behind.

This benefit gets paid once a week or month; you can apply via the HMRC app and even backdate it for three months. So, if you are someone who hasn't applied for child benefit and your children are older than three months, you might be losing money.

There is an earnings threshold; if you earn above a certain amount, you start to lose the benefit. You can choose to opt out of receiving the payments and still complete the application to protect your national insurance contributions or pass them along to someone else.

There is a child benefit tax calculator available on the HMRC website, so it's worth checking it out. Child benefit payments are made every four weeks, with £25.60 allocated for the first child and £16.95 for each additional child. There's no limit to the number of children you can claim for.

Over the course of a child's life from birth to age 16, this benefit can go beyond £20,000. Additionally, when you claim child benefit, your child is automatically issued a national insurance number, and the years you are actively claiming child benefit count as years tallied towards your state pension eligibility. However, eligibility and payment amounts are based on your net adjusted income, which includes taxable earnings like bonuses and commissions but excludes deductions for Gift Aid donations, pension contributions and similar allowances.

The Sure Start Maternity Grant offers £500 to help with the costs of having a child. However, this grant is only available for your first child, and while there's no specific income threshold, you must be receiving certain benefits such as Universal Credit. You need to apply within 11 weeks before your due date or up to six months after your baby is born.

Student loan repayments: If your income drops below the repayment threshold, your student loan repayments should automatically stop. You are not required to make repayments until your income rises above the annual threshold again. However, if repayments were deducted during a period when you earned below the threshold, you may be eligible for a refund. Log into your Student Loans Company (SLC) account to request a refund. While reclaiming overpaid amounts gives you the money back, it's worth noting that it also increases the total outstanding balance on your loan.

Marriage allowance: If your income drops below the personal allowance threshold (£12,570 for the current tax year), you can transfer up to £1,260 of your unused personal allowance to your partner. This reduces their tax bill by £252 over the year. To be eligible, you must be married or in a civil partnership, and your partner's income must be under £50,270. You can apply for the marriage allowance online using both of your National Insurance numbers.

THINGS YOU NEED TO REMEMBER:

- You can earn up to £1,000 a year from side hustles without needing to report it to HMRC, but anything over that is taxable.

- From renting out a room to selling online or freelancing, there are multiple ways to generate extra income beyond your main job.

- If your side hustle grows in frequency or intention (like buying to sell for profit), it may cross the line into becoming a business, requiring self-employment registration and tax filing.

PART FOUR
Managing your Money

Now that we've covered the foundations of your income and explored additional ways to earn, it's time to focus on managing the money you bring in. Part 4 is about taking control of your finances and setting up systems to keep your money working for you, not the other way around. From budgeting and saving to borrowing and spending wisely, this section provides practical strategies to make the most of that hard-earned money you've brought in.

We'll start by auditing your money with a look at budgeting techniques that can help you align your finances with your goals. Next, we'll dig into the essentials of saving and borrowing, covering everything from emergency funds and ISAs to credit cards and loans. You'll learn how to assess when borrowing makes sense and when it might be better to hold off.

We'll also tackle the everyday choices that impact your financial health, like spending habits, how to make the most of your money when buying or renting, and tips for avoiding unnecessary costs. Managing money isn't just about tracking where it goes; it's about building a plan that gives you the freedom to live life on your terms.

By the end of this part, you'll have a toolkit of strategies to confidently navigate your finances, helping you take charge of your money and lay the groundwork for a stable financial future.

8. Budgeting your Money

Let's talk about budgeting; don't worry, it's not as daunting as it sounds. Whether you're paid by an employer or running your own show, establishing a few solid habits on payday can transform your financial outlook. Think of budgeting as a financial tune-up, helping you keep your money working as hard as you do. It's not about restrictions; it's about empowerment, making intentional choices with every pound you have.

Imagine I'm your financial auditor, guiding you through a straightforward audit of your life. Once we've done this a few times together, you'll be in control and might even find yourself teaching someone else how to do it. Because that's all budgeting is; it's about creating habits that build a strong foundation for your financial success, not about following strict rules or spreadsheets.

We'll explore different budgeting methods like the 50/30/20 rule, zero-based budgeting and more. But here's the thing: no single approach guarantees success. Real success comes from knowing how to manage your money like an accountant would, but without the endless spreadsheets. We'll cover everything, from what to do on payday to picking the right bank accounts so your money flows exactly where it needs to go.

Budgeting is about choice; it empowers you to afford what matters without trying to afford everything. It's about making sure your money aligns with what's most important to you. So, let's break it down step by step.

A financial audit

If you think of budgeting like auditing your life, it starts to feel more manageable, right? The key is setting aside time to review your finances and being honest with yourself about where your money is going. Don't think of it as a one-time thing; think of it as creating habits that will keep you on track. The best part? Once you get into the rhythm, you'll feel more in control, and it becomes second nature.

Here's how we'll get started:

Gather your accounts

Start by gathering everything: current accounts, credit cards, savings accounts, loans and any investment accounts. Think of this as your financial inventory.

Download your statements

Collect your bank statements and credit card bills, and take a close look at your spending over the past few months. To make this easier and more insightful, try grouping your expenses into categories like dining out, clothing, travel, groceries and entertainment. It might seem overwhelming, but categorising helps you clearly see where your money is going, a crucial foundation for effective budgeting. You don't have to have hundreds of categories, even just necessities vs. nice-to-haves is a useful categorisation system.

Review and reflect

As you go through your statements, note where your money is going; look at this monthly first as an easier step, then go wider. What patterns do you see? Are there unexpected expenses popping up? Are your daily lattes adding up more than you thought? And are you OK with this? It's all part of understanding your financial habits.

Calculate your net worth

Your net worth is the difference between what you own (your assets) and what you owe (your liabilities). It's a good way to get an overall view of your financial health. Don't worry if it's not where you want it to be; this is just the starting point. It can be scary to see these numbers for the first time, but it's imperative we have an understanding of our situation to improve; ignorance is not bliss in this situation.

Budgeting methods

Now that you've got a clearer picture of your finances let's look at a few budgeting methods. There's no one-size-fits-all, so try out a few and see what fits your lifestyle best:

Envelope budgeting (zero-based budgeting)

This method involves assigning every pound a purpose. You 'spend' all your income on paper by dividing it into categories like rent, groceries and savings until you hit zero. The idea is that you give every pound a job before you spend it.

Value-based budgeting

With this approach, you prioritise spending on the things that matter most to you, cutting out the rest. It's about aligning your money with your values, whether that's travel, investing in education or saving for a home.

The 50/30/20 rule

This popular rule suggests you divide your income into three categories: 50 per cent for needs (like rent and groceries), 30 per cent for wants (like dining out or Netflix), and 20 per cent for savings or debt repayment. It's a simple formula that works for many, but feel free to tweak it based on your own lifestyle as for many early on in their career they might find 50 per cent for their needs is too low as covering rent alone in a city in the UK could be almost half the average graduate salary; conversely, as you get close to retirement your needs might be reduced if you've paid off your mortgage and therefore don't have to cover that on a month-to-month basis.

After mapping out your financial landscape and choosing a budgeting method, it's time to put that plan into action. A key part of staying on track financially is mastering your payday routine. Payday isn't just when money arrives in your account; it's a checkpoint to take charge of your budget and make sure each pound has a purpose. This way, you won't just 'hope' your budget works; you'll actively manage it, setting yourself up for financial success every month.

What you should do on payday

Payday can feel both exciting and overwhelming. It's easy to let automatic deductions flow out for rent, bills and essentials while keeping an eye on what's left. But often, that 'leftover' money disappears before we even realise it. Let's change that up. Instead of watching your money trickle away, let's put a plan in place to take control.

Once you've confirmed your pay matches your expectations, you're ready to direct each part of it intentionally. Here's a step-by-step guide for maximising payday:

Allocate to essentials

Once your money lands in your account, immediately allocate funds to your essential spending, such as rent, mortgage and bills. Suppose these are set up as direct debits. That's great! But take a moment to mentally or physically track what's been paid and what's coming out soon.

Automate your savings

Before you do anything else, pay yourself. Set up an automatic transfer to your savings or investment account. By automating it, you ensure that you're building wealth before spending on non-essentials. Whether it's 10 per cent, 20 per cent, or more, this habit will give you peace of mind and financial stability.

Track your spending

Don't just hope your money will last until the next payday. Use a budgeting app, spreadsheet or even a notebook to keep tabs on where it's going. Whether you're using the 50/30/20 rule or your own system, tracking helps you stick to your plan and adjust where needed.

Create 'spending buckets'

Divide your remaining money into categories, like entertainment and birthday gifts, so you know exactly how much you can spend in each area. This prevents the 'leftover' money from disappearing into thin air.

Stress-test your budget

Consider what would happen if an unexpected expense or a dip in income occurred. Building a buffer into your budget for unplanned costs gives you extra security, helping you stay on track when things don't go as planned.

Once you've allocated funds to essentials, automated your savings, and created spending buckets, the next step is to make sure you have the right bank accounts in place to support these efforts. The accounts you choose can make a big difference in how effectively you manage your money. Having the right structure and tools is crucial, whether it's dividing funds between spending, bills and savings or ensuring that every account is working toward your goals.

Which bank accounts make sense for you

Let's dig into the accounts that can streamline your financial life. A lot of people stick with the account they opened as a teenager without considering if it's still serving them well. But your bank accounts should work for you; think of them as your financial 'A-team'. Each account should have a purpose, helping you manage different parts of your financial life smoothly and efficiently.

With current accounts, you might have pots like:

- House pot – mortgage or rent
- Bills pot
- Wedding pot
- Fun pot
- Emergency fund
- Savings accounts
  - ISAs
  - General savings
  - Shared savings accounts
- Investment account
- Long-term savings/pension accounts (you might not have this)
- Holiday accounts – like Christmas or Chinese New Year
- Side-hustle income

Where is your money going once you have it? Your bank account? If this is the one you opened in senior school that you've just stayed with, out of loyalty, we need to talk.

Your bank accounts should look like the ultimate team of cards – imagine the Avengers – who are furiously working for you. If you're wondering if they are or not, they aren't.

We're going to go through the bank account that works for you and determine how much you need to set yourself up for success. We have a full chapter on savings coming up, so this is mainly about current accounts.

These should all come with tons of benefits. Banks are not like partners; it's not disloyal to shop around. It's actively encouraged. They are all competing to give you the best, and so they should be; your money is valuable, and they need it. More and more initiatives are coming in to keep them competitive, and we need to be involved in the process so banks don't feel like we've let them off the hook.

Your current account is where your money starts its journey. From there, it might move to your savings, investments or even cover nights out or a new car. Money flows in and out, circulating as you spend and save. But often, where it first arrives seems unimportant, similar to how some people view their car as just a way to get from point A to point B. However, choosing the right current account can actually benefit you financially, much like upgrading from an old, worn-out car to something more reliable. If you stick with the same account you opened years ago without considering alternatives, you might be missing out on opportunities to make your money work harder for you.

The current account is designed to have money

flowing through it constantly; you get salaries paid in here, you pay out for lunch, and you even take cash out of this account. It's probably the most frequently used type of account.

I have some rules:

1. If the app and website are easy to use, you're halfway there; if they are not, WALK AWAY. In this day and age, there is literally zero excuse for a bank not to have an easy-to-use website and app.

2. Customer service: We never want to use it, but we want to feel confident that it's easy to get hold of someone and they can offer genuine support when it's required. I've sat on phone lines or battled chatbots online that made me want to scream, and again, in this era, we shouldn't stand for it.

3. Fees: We should never see fees on current accounts unless you can see the benefit outweighing the fee.

And finally, protecting your money is where the £85,000 rule comes in handy. The Financial Services Compensation Scheme (FSCS) ensures that if your bank or building society goes bust, your money is protected up to £85,000 per financial institution. So, if you've got your hard-earned cash tucked away in a current account, you can rest easy knowing that up to £85,000 of your money is safe, even if the worst happens. This means that if you have more than £85,000, it would be worth spreading your money across different banks to make sure all your money is covered. It's like having a financial safety net, ensuring your funds are protected without any complicated fuss.

As we spoke about banks in Chapter 3, you'll know this is unlikely to happen out of nowhere. Banks in the UK only have to discuss takeovers for the media to go mad, so if a bank were to fail it is unlikely to happen as a big surprise. But as some people found out during the 2022 collapse of the cryptocurrency company FTX, this protection could have come into play to support them had FTX been a UK institution.

How to sit back and watch your money move

Dolce far niente – she says, pretending she's Julia Roberts – is the sweetness of doing nothing; that is the end goal. The ability to know that every month, every week, or whenever you want it to happen, your money is moving around to work for you. A blissful lifestyle is really what we want. We don't want to be accountants or finance experts; we just want money to work itself out for us. Unfortunately, to get to that bliss, you have to put in the graft up front.

If you've got a workplace pension, congratulations, you're already dipping your toes into automation. Before your salary hits your bank account, your employer automatically deducts a percentage and deposits it into your pension. You didn't have to think about it; it's all done behind the scenes. The payroll software is doing the heavy lifting, sorting everything out without your input. That's exactly the type of automation we want for your personal finances. Imagine every part of your money management running like clockwork, all on autopilot.

The costs we know

Let's start with the non-negotiable costs – which you can predict to the penny. This is your rent or mortgage, your utility bills, maybe your council tax or phone bill. You can probably tell me the exact day these payments come out each month.

These are the first things to automate. Why? Because these payments are the backbone of your financial stability, and they should never be left to chance. You don't want to be scrambling at 11.55pm trying to remember your online banking password to pay the rent. Instead, set up a standing order from your current account. These are recurring payments, and you can programme them to go out on the same day every month. That way, whether you're sipping cocktails on holiday or knee-deep in a work project, your bills are paid without you lifting a finger.

Next up are your savings and investments. Set up automatic transfers for your emergency fund, your high-yield savings account, and any investment accounts you've opened. Decide how much goes into each pot and when, and then let your bank do the rest. If you've got a savings goal, whether that's a holiday, a house or just a rainy-day fund, automation makes sure you're contributing to it regularly without even thinking about it.

The key is consistency. Every time money comes in, it should go back out into the right places to set you up for a secure financial future.

The costs we have no idea are coming

Now, what about the costs we can't predict? That unexpected car repair, the forgotten birthday gift (sorry, Mum) or the random expense that pops up just when you least expect it? This is why automating contributions to an emergency fund is so crucial. An emergency fund is your financial buffer or your safety net. Automating even a small amount each month into an easy-access savings account will help protect you when life throws you a curveball.

So, when the unexpected happens (and it always will), you're prepared, and it doesn't derail the rest of your financial plans.

Automation is about creating a system where you don't have to worry about every single detail because the important stuff is handled in the background. You're not just hoping your money is in the right place; you're making sure of it. So, take the time to set up your own financial automation system, and before long you'll be enjoying that *dolce far niente* without stressing about what's in your bank account.

THINGS YOU NEED TO REMEMBER:

- Rather than restricting, budgeting gives you the power to direct your money towards what matters most to you, setting you up for financial success. Use methods like the 50/30/20 rule or zero-based budgeting – find a system that works with your goals.

- Take control of payday by ensuring everything aligns with your expectations, then allocate funds immediately to essentials, automate your savings and set spending limits. This structure prevents your hard-earned money from slipping away unnoticed.

- Different accounts or 'money pots' can simplify managing your finances. Setting up separate pots for bills, savings and even fun spending allows you to ensure every pound has a purpose, making budgeting more intuitive and effective.

9. Savings

Now that you've set your foundations with budgeting, it's time to look at the next step in managing your money: saving. Think of savings as your safety blanket. They don't have to be massive, and they may fluctuate over time, but having them can make all the difference when life throws you a curveball. In this chapter, we'll explore different saving options, from ISAs to premium bonds, and strategies to build both short- and long-term goals. Plus, we'll touch on ways to save smartly while minimising the tax you pay. Because, yes, savings can come with tax implications – sorry about that!

Building a savings habit is about preparing for the 'what ifs' in life. Whether it's an emergency fund, holiday savings or a cushion for unexpected life changes, your savings give you stability and security. If you think back to Chapter 2, savings are one of those positive financial habits that reduce stress and bring peace of mind.

Life is uncertain, and there are a million reasons why you need to prepare through savings:

- You're in a job you hate, and you want to leave
- Your relationship has become unhealthy
- Your car breaks down

- Medically, you need support fast
- In a twist of fate, a picture hanging in your living room falls, smashing your new TV, knocking over a cherished vase and ruining a freshly dry-cleaned dress on the sofa nearby. Do you see where I'm going with this? Life has a fun way of reminding you that you're not always in control.

But you *are* in control of how you efficiently manage your money, and saving is part of that. It can be a brilliant way to quieten your mind when you start to panic that you're not where you thought you would be in life. When your safety blanket is in place, and you put it there, you can pat your younger self on the back for sorting it out.

General savings accounts

When it comes to savings, there are a few key things to look for to find the right account: access, interest and the bank itself. First, how easily can you dip into your savings? Is the account flexible, or do you need to give notice? Then there's interest: how much is your money growing while it sits there? And finally, the bank or building society: do they work for you? Is their app or website easy to use? Are they ethically good?

Access

Savings accounts, in general, come in a variety of forms:

1. Easy access: Where you can withdraw your money at any time whenever you need it without penalties.
2. Fixed-term accounts: These require you to lock your money away for a set period – 30 days, six months, a year or longer – in exchange for higher interest rates.
3. Notice accounts: Accounts that require you to give a certain amount of notice (e.g. 30 days) before making a withdrawal.

Interest rates

The interest rate on your savings account determines how much you earn on your money, and it's crucial to pay attention to this. We will touch on interest rates again when we discuss debt in Chapter 10, and the same rules apply there. Ideally, your savings should earn a rate close to or above the Bank of England's base rate. When base rates are low, don't be surprised if your savings account offers a pretty poor return. But when rates rise, shop around for better options.

Now, this interest you earn is considered income. If it exceeds your personal savings allowance of £1k (if you are a basic-rate income tax payer – see Chapter 6), you will need to pay tax on it. The bank will notify HMRC, but it's ultimately your responsibility to declare it through a self-assessment, which needs to be done by 5 October after the end of the tax year. If you're earning above your allowance, HMRC will adjust your tax code accordingly.

Remember, general savings accounts aren't tax-free like ISAs, but we'll cover those in more detail in the next part.

Choosing either a bank or building society

Just like with current accounts, your savings account doesn't have to be with the first bank you think of. Explore building societies, high street banks and even online-only banks, which often have better interest rates and lower fees. We have covered this already, but I think it's valuable I reiterate the message: banks are publicly traded, meaning they have shareholders whose primary goal is to make profits. That often means their product offerings are designed with profit in mind.

Building societies, on the other hand, are mutual organisations. This means they're owned by their members and customers like you, so their priority is often on providing better rates and customer service rather than just generating profits.

Savings pots, aka emergency-fund pots or 'goals' pots

Think of savings as your financial foundation. This is the bedrock that supports your entire financial life. Whether it's an emergency fund or a savings pot for future goals, these accounts should be easily accessible so that you don't have to dip into investments in a pinch. Trying to pull money out of long-term investments in a hurry could mean selling at a loss, something we all want to avoid.

So, how much should you save? Your foundation should be big enough to handle life's curveballs but not so large that it holds you back from making more productive investments. It's all about balance; your savings need to be there for emergencies, but you shouldn't sit idle for too long.

Check in with your savings goals at least once a year to make sure they're still in line with your financial situation. Has your emergency fund grown too large? Or maybe you need to top it up? Keep it flexible and adjust it to fit your evolving goals. Your savings are a powerful tool. When used correctly, they provide stability and open up opportunities for building your financial future.

ISAs

Individual savings accounts were created in 1999 by then-chancellor Gordon Brown to stimulate savings for the everyday person. They replaced earlier tax-free savings accounts known as personal equity plans (PEPs) and tax-exempt special savings accounts (TESSAs).

The rules are that you have a £20,000 annual allowance for your ISA per tax year, and this is a use-it-or lose-it scheme. Once you've saved your £20k or the tax year ends, you can't go back and use any unused allowance.

Any interest or other income earned in an ISA is tax-free, so there's no income tax, dividend tax or capital gains tax to be paid on anything. When you have used up the allowance, that's it, and if you take the money out, you do lose your allowance, which is why if you need to move money from one ISA to another it is important to always do it as a transfer and let your bank know that you're going to move your money; don't just drain one account and open another.

You can build up more than £20k in an account; it's just the allowance in the year that is capped. However, there isn't just one kind of ISA. There are four adult ISA varieties and one for children. You used to only be allowed one of each type, but now you can have as many as you like, but it's important to remember you don't have £20k per account; the allowance is split across them. If you go over the allowance the bank will flag this to you and to HMRC, who will ask you to resolve the situation or ask your bank to move the excess funds to a general savings account.

Each of those four adult ISAs has their own nuances, so let's dive in:

1. Cash ISA: The most well-known of the individual
   savings accounts, the cash ISA, is very similar to
   a general savings account. The only difference is
   that any interest earned in a cash ISA is tax-free.

You can put up to £20,000 a year into your cash ISA.
The cash ISA is ideal for savers who like stability
and offers a range of options, from easy access to flexible withdrawals and fixed-rate accounts, which might
offer you higher interest for leaving your money in the
account for a longer period of time.

Cash ISAs are also protected by the FSCS up to £85k
per bank or building society, adding an extra layer of
protection to your savings.

2. Lifetime ISA: Introduced in April 2017, lifetime
   ISAs (LISAs) were designed to help people
   save for their first home or retirement. These
   accounts offer a government bonus. Each tax
   year, you can contribute up to £4,000 into a
   LISA, and the government will boost your
   savings by 25 per cent, adding up to £1,000
   annually. This means that every £4 you save
   turns into £5, making it an attractive option
   for long-term savers.

It's important to note that this contribution limit is
part of your overall £20,000 annual ISA allowance, so it
reduces the amount you can put into other ISAs in the
same year.

LISAs can be opened by individuals aged 18 to 40 (actually 39 and 364 days), and you can start with as little as £1. The primary purpose of a LISA is to help first-time buyers, but it can also be used as a retirement fund. If you're using it to buy your first home, there are a few conditions to meet:

- The property must be your first-ever home purchase.
- The home must cost £450,000 or less.
- The account must be open for at least 12 months before using it for a home purchase.

For those not purchasing a home, LISAs can serve as an additional retirement savings tool. You can withdraw the funds tax-free once you turn 60, providing another tax-efficient way to save for the future.

However, there is a significant consideration to keep in mind: if you withdraw funds from a Lifetime ISA for reasons other than purchasing your first home or reaching age 60, you will incur a withdrawal penalty. This penalty is currently set at 25 per cent, which not only reclaims the government bonus but also imposes an additional charge on your original savings. This means careful planning is essential to avoid unnecessary penalties and to make the most of the LISA benefits.

3. Stocks and shares ISA: This is also referred to as an investment ISA because you can invest in other products, not just stocks and shares. It is the

tax-efficient way to open an investment account
that allows you to invest without paying any tax
on income such as dividends or capital gains.

The annual allowance of £20k could be used entirely
in a stocks and shares ISA, but to reiterate, if you use
any of your annual allowance in another ISA, it reduces
the amount you have to invest in an S&S ISA.

We will get into what types of investments are on
offer in Chapter 13, but there isn't a stopper on what
can be invested in the S&S ISA: exchange-traded funds,
bonds, commodities, etc.

4. Innovative finance ISA: The least common of
   the ISAs, the IFISA, allows you to lend money
   to others in a peer-to-peer lending scheme.
   It was introduced in 2016 to stimulate people
   to lend to other people or businesses, with the
   lender receiving interest in return.

When interest rates are low, such as when the Bank
of England has a base rate of 1 per cent, people see
innovative finance ISA rates of 7 per cent to 12 per cent
and think these returns are guaranteed and better than
they're getting, so they jump at the opportunity.

However, these peer-to-peer lending schemes are investments, and therefore, there is no guarantee you'll get the 7
per cent as a minimum, and unlike other bank accounts,
there is no safety from the FSCS protection scheme.

Peer-to-peer lending is where you lend your money,

and that money is split between businesses and personal loans that all give you a different interest rate. The 7.5 per cent is the average of the basket of investments. All it takes is for one of those businesses or personal loans to go bankrupt and default on their loan, and that interest starts going down.

This is by far the riskiest of all of the ISAs; you can, in theory, put all of your £20k ISA tax allowance into an innovative finance ISA, but most providers won't let you put this amount in if you haven't invested this way before.

Things to check include how your provider protects your money and the minimum sum you can lend. Check the platform's track record on defaults and losses. These loans have terms, so is there a way to get the cash out?

These should be compared against investments, like the stocks and shares ISA described below – but instead of investing in a stock of (for example) Tesla, you're lending your money to companies and people who might not be able to get this funding elsewhere, and this is a risk you do need to consider.

Which to choose?

There are a ton of providers when it comes to stocks and shares ISAs, but here are some of the things I'd look for:

1. Low fees or zero fees: Sometimes, if you're being charged for having the ISA open, you might find

your gains or dividend income is being eaten up each month by the fees, so you're making nothing.

2. Access: You want a provider who gives you good access to investments you're interested in, such as specific stocks and shares or a type of bond.

3. Education: In this day and age, there is no excuse for the providers to make anything complicated. They should have easy to watch, read or even listen to explanations of what is going on.

4. A good platform: Look for one that's user-friendly, intuitive and accessible on both mobile and desktop. It should offer tools for tracking your investments and portfolio performance, along with easy navigation for buying and selling.

Certain investment platforms suit some people better than others. Some of them also love a bit of pinkwashing to make women feel more seen, which is fine, but just be aware of others out there.

On the risk scale, stocks and shares ISAs probably come just below innovative finance ISAs because, unlike cash ISAs, where you may get a guaranteed return, these are investments. As we will discuss, the market is volatile, and with investments, it's about playing the long-term game.

5. I did say there were four adult ISAs, and there is a fifth, but this is just for children. It's called the junior ISA: Junior ISAs are designed for children from birth to age 18.

A junior ISA is restricted to £9k per child per tax year. It can be opened by a guardian for anyone under 18. At 16, the child can actually turn this into a cash ISA if they so wish. A junior ISA can be either a cash ISA, earning interest, or an S&S ISA where the guardian invests the money on their behalf.

All income earned in a junior ISA, like the adult accounts, is tax-free. Many banks are aware that this money is tied up for 16 to 18 years, and therefore there are good rates to be had on these accounts. As we saw in Chapter 3, banks use our money to lend to others, and if they can guarantee you're not going to be taking your money out because you legally can't, then they know they can invest it for longer periods of time.

There are non-ISA accounts for children, and children do have a personal allowance themselves, but if a guardian is funding the child's account and they earn more than £100 in interest, it's taxed as if it's the guardian's income.

Will we ever get more types of ISAs?

In 2024, Rishi Sunak's government floated the idea of a British ISA; this would give you an extra £5k on top of your £20k allowance but only to be invested in British-backed equities (stocks and shares).

Investment platforms weren't keen on it and didn't see how it would work in practice. The idea was scrapped; however, it did bring to light the question of whether reform is needed across the ISAs in play.

The LISA, for instance, could be adjusted to increase the value of the home it can be used to buy, or the cash ISA could have better benefits than just standard interest. A general rise in the £20k allowance wouldn't go amiss.

Premium bonds

With the word 'bond' in the name, you'd be forgiven for thinking premium bonds belong in the investment chapter. But as you'll soon discover, these aren't the guaranteed-returns kind of bond you might expect. However, what they do offer is liquidity, meaning you can quickly turn them back into cash and safety, as they're backed by the government through National Savings and Investments (NS&I).

Premium bonds have long been seen as a bit of an old-school savings choice. Chances are, if you ask your parents or grandparents, they probably had one bought for them by a relative. And while they went out of fashion for a while, they've made quite the comeback recently, thanks to a combination of rising interest in safe savings options and a bit of that thrill-of-the-prize allure of the jackpot.

Each person can hold up to £50,000 in Premium Bonds, and every £1 you put in has an equal chance of winning in the monthly prize draw. There are two £1 million jackpots every month, and while the odds may not be in your favour with smaller amounts, you might still win! Of course, with a higher balance, your chances increase. Thirty-eight out of the last 100 million-pound winners had the full £50k invested. But to keep it interesting, someone with just £17 in bonds walked away with £1 million back in 2004, proving that even a little can go a long way, if you're very lucky.

The current underlying rate of return is 4.2 per cent, which is just an average figure; don't mistake it for a guaranteed interest rate. Some people will do much better; many will walk away with nothing. You could win a range of prizes from £25 to £1 million, and that possibility of life-changing sums is a big part of the appeal.

> Good to know: You can buy premium bonds on the NS&I website (www.nsandi.com). You set up an account in your name and purchase bonds; to get your money back, you can sell them back to NS&I, and it will sell your oldest bonds first.

Despite the odds, premium bonds remain incredibly popular, with more than 124 billion bonds in circulation today. People love them for the thrill they offer, like a lottery where you don't lose your money if you don't win. You've still got your original investment sitting there, safe and sound, ready to withdraw if you need it. In fact, the average bondholder has about £5,250 invested[3], and around a million people have maxed out their £50k limit[4].

That's part of the fun. There's always that chance of winning big. As journalist Lee Boyce reportedly said, 'Money isn't fun in general, but premium bonds make saving a little more exciting.' And when it comes to savings, we should absolutely take the excitement where we can find it!

Why premium bonds? Let's be real: even with some of the best savings accounts offering interest rates of over 5 per cent, none of them give you the chance to win £1 million. That's why people are drawn to them; it's the blend of safety, liquidity and that little bit of excitement.

But remember, it's all about balance. Diversify your savings. Premium bonds are a great part of the picture, but they shouldn't be your only plan. Spread your money across different savings and investment options to maximise your chances of growing wealth; don't rely on the hope of a big win.

THINGS YOU NEED TO REMEMBER:

- Don't rely on just one account. Mix general savings, ISAs and premium bonds for a balanced approach.

- ISAs offer tax-free savings, so make the most of your annual allowance to protect your earnings.

- While not guaranteed, premium bonds offer the thrill of winning big without risking your initial savings.

10. Borrowing Money

Borrowing money, when approached with intention and understanding, can be a valuable tool for building the life you want. Whether it's using a credit card for everyday purchases, taking out a student loan to invest in your future, or accessing a short-term loan during an emergency, borrowing allows you to seize opportunities and bridge financial gaps when you need to. It's not just a necessity; it's a strategy.

Consider this: some of the biggest milestones in life, such as buying a home, pursuing higher education or even starting your own business, are often made possible through borrowing.

Managed well, debt can be the stepping stone to achieving goals that might otherwise seem out of reach. However, when borrowing is misunderstood or misused, it can quickly become a burden. That's why the key isn't to avoid debt entirely but to borrow with purpose and knowledge.

One of the largest and most common forms of borrowing you'll likely face is a mortgage, which we'll cover in detail in Chapter 12. This chapter, however, focuses on the more everyday types of borrowing that are just as important to understand.

The world of borrowing comes with its own language, terms like APR (annual percentage rate) and LTV (loan-to-value ratio). At first, it can feel overwhelming, but once you grasp these concepts, they stop being intimidating and instead become tools you can use to make smarter financial decisions. For example, understanding APR isn't just about numbers; it's about saving money. APR reflects the total cost of borrowing over a year, including interest and fees, and knowing how to compare APRs can save you hundreds, if not thousands, of pounds. Choosing the right LTV ratio on a mortgage could mean lower monthly payments and less overall interest.

By the end of this chapter, you won't just know the difference between good and bad debt; you'll understand how to approach borrowing as an opportunity rather than an obligation. This is your guide to borrowing with purpose, managing debt wisely, and using it as a tool to build a financially secure future.

Are there good or bad debts?

Not all debts are created equal. Debt is simply a way to borrow money, but the purpose and terms of that borrowing can vary drastically. Whether it's a mortgage, a student loan or a credit card, debt can serve different purposes. Sometimes it's referred to as leverage, which is just a fancy term for borrowing money to invest in something that could make you more money in the future. But not every debt qualifies as leverage.

Think of debt as existing on a personal spectrum. For some people, a certain type of debt might fall into the 'good' category, while for others, the same debt could be a ticking time bomb. If you're savvy with your finances, you can use debt to your advantage. Think low-interest mortgages or student loans that fund a degree with high earning potential. On the flip side, if managing debt isn't your strong suit, those same loans could feel like a weight dragging you down.

Your mindset and financial habits play a huge role here. Some people view all debt as negative, a mindset shaped by past experiences or beliefs. Others see 'good debt' as an investment in their future. For example, a student loan for a degree with strong career prospects might be a smart move, while racking up debt for a holiday could be more of a burden. But context matters: for someone else, that holiday debt might be worth it for the mental recharge it provides, while a degree they don't end up using might feel like a financial setback.

In short, debt isn't just about numbers; it's about how that debt impacts you and your financial well-being. Knowing where you stand on that spectrum will help you decide which debts are worth taking on and which ones you should avoid until you're more prepared.

Credit cards

While a debit card is used to spend your own money, a credit card is essentially a short-term loan. You borrow from a financial institution each month. If managed well, credit cards can actually reward you – with air miles, cashback and added purchase protection.

Credit cards first came to the UK in 1966, but the modern concept we're familiar with didn't fully take off until 1989. Although credit cards might seem relatively new, the idea of credit has been around for centuries.

Many people rush to get the same flashy card their friends have or one that makes a statement when splitting a bill, but that doesn't mean it's the right card for you. Credit cards can be powerful financial tools, acting as a free short-term loan when managed well. They can also become a financial headache if misused. So, let's break down what they are, how to choose the right one, and what you need to know about things like credit limits, interest rates and your credit score.

What are credit cards?

Credit cards are issued by financial institutions, giving you a line of credit you can borrow against as a cardholder. The key difference between a credit and a debit card is that with a credit card, you're spending borrowed money that you'll pay back, while with a debit card, you're using money that's already in your account.

When you're approved for a credit card, you'll receive a credit limit; this is the maximum amount you can borrow. For example, if you're given a £1,000 credit limit, you can spend up to £1,000 that month. Once you've repaid the balance, you can borrow again up to your limit. If you spend £500, you'll still have £500 left to use until you pay off what you owe.

Next, there's the interest rate, known as the APR (annual percentage rate). Ideally, you want to avoid paying any interest at all, as credit card APRs are typically sky-high, often over 20 per cent. Interest only kicks in if you don't pay off your balance in full by the end of the month (unless you have a 0 per cent APR or special offer). To avoid this, set up a direct debit that pays off the total balance from your current account every month. This way, you're essentially getting a free loan each month without paying a penny in interest.

When should I get a credit card?

You're legally allowed to get a credit card at 18, but whether you *should* is another question. I hear from students all the time that as soon as they turn 18, their inbox is flooded with offers for credit cards, loans and overdrafts. It can be tempting, like having 'free' money waved in front of you, but it's not free, and it comes with strings attached.

In my opinion, there should be stricter rules around offering financial products to young adults. Think about it: student loans are means tested based on your parents' income because the government doesn't consider you fully financially independent. Yet financial institutions are more than happy to hand out credit products that could impact your credit score and financial future before you've had a chance to understand them properly.

A good credit card, though, can save you money in more ways than one. Not only can you earn rewards like cashback on your purchases or points, but a well-managed credit card can boost your credit score. A healthy credit score means access to other types of borrowing, like loans and mortgages, at lower interest rates, potentially saving you thousands over your lifetime.

When considering if you need a credit card, ask yourself the following:

1. Do you understand that credit is borrowed money that you must pay back each month? Credit isn't free money; it's a loan, and if you don't pay it back, there are consequences. If you're unsure how this works, don't worry; we'll cover it in detail later.

2. Do you realise that only paying the minimum amount each month means paying interest on what you've borrowed? Paying the minimum might seem like an easy way out, but it's a trap. You'll start accruing interest on the balance,

often at high rates, which can lead to mounting debt over time.

3. Will the credit card work for you? A credit card should be a tool that gives you benefits, whether that's cashback, air miles or another type of reward. If your card isn't offering you anything in return for using it, shop for another one.

4. Do you see it as a way to boost your credit score but understand that it can also harm your score if not used responsibly? A credit card can help build a healthy credit history if used wisely. But it's a double-edged sword; missing a payment or overspending can drag your score down, making it harder to get loans or mortgages in the future.

5. Is your income stable enough to support the use of a credit card? Just because you're eligible for a card doesn't mean it's affordable for you. Lenders consider your income when offering credit, and if your income is low or unstable, you may struggle to manage the debt.

But this does not mean you absolutely have to have a credit card. If you're someone who just doesn't like the idea of having something that you've got to remember to pay off each month, you don't want to set up the automation, or you just don't feel like a credit card, that's absolutely fine; it's not a mandatory requirement for being an adult.

How do I know the credit card I have is right for me?

Is it giving you something back? That is the minimum the credit card should be doing, whether it's through air miles, cashback or something else. Your credit card should be working with you, not against you.

Something to also consider is that not all institutions will take certain types of credit cards. Many businesses won't take American Express because of the charges they incur for accepting it.

What to look for when deciding which credit card to go for

What are you getting from them?

- Cashback
- Points
- Travel perks like airport lounge access and late checkout in hotels
- Insurance

These are all very real perks, and if you're thinking, *I have a credit card and don't get any of these*, I'd say it's time to move. If you search online for credit cards, there are tons of sites ready to help you find the one that suits you and your lifestyle.

What is a credit score?

Think of your credit score like a school report card. Remember how you had homework, tests and projects that all contributed to your final grade at the end of the year? Your credit score works in a similar way. It's a summary of all your financial behaviour over time, added up to create one score that lenders use to decide if they should lend you money. Every financial move you make, whether it's paying your bills on time or taking out a loan, gets added to your credit file, and that file is used to build a picture of how 'creditworthy' you are.

In the UK, there isn't just one big boss of credit scores. Instead, there are three main credit rating agencies: Experian, TransUnion and Equifax. Each of these agencies gives you a score based on your financial activity, but here's the catch: they don't all score you in the exact same way. One agency might give you a higher score than another because they have slightly different ways of calculating it.

Lenders, like banks and credit card companies, use your credit score (and sometimes their own internal criteria) to decide if they should lend to you, how much to lend, and at what interest rate. Your score is essentially their way of assessing how likely you are to repay the money you borrow.

It's important to remember that your score isn't static; it can change over time based on your financial behaviour. Just like in school, if you work hard and manage your finances responsibly, your score will reflect that. But if you miss payments or take on too much debt, it can drop. So, think of your credit score as a reflection of your financial habits; like all habits, they can be improved.

Ways you could be boosting or harming your score!

Your score is not fixed; it is all about trust. Have you been around long enough for financial institutions to trust you? Do they know you? If you're 'brilliant' with money but have never interacted with banks, they will still find it hard to trust you because they don't know anything.

Ways you can boost your score:

- Registering to vote – and remembering to do this whenever you move.
- A low debt ratio – aim to keep your unsecured debt (debt not tied to an asset, such as non-mortgage or non-student loan debt) below 20 per cent of your annual income.
- Keep credit utilisation low – the percentage of available credit used. Suppose you have £100 of debt on a card with a £1k limit that is 10 per cent. So, having more available credit can improve your credit score without you using it.
- Length of credit history – this will come up again as a way that can harm your score, but a long credit history has a positive impact.
- Make payments on time – in full.

Things that could be bringing your score down:

- Closing credit card accounts – closing down accounts can harm your score, especially if you've had them for a long time. Your credit history starts with the oldest card on your list, and if you close the account, the history can be halved.
  - Credit rating agencies and lenders are looking for 'evidence of stability'. I have two credit cards, one of which I got when I was 19; honestly, because I thought that's what I 'should' do, I barely used it for fear of being sucked into the credit abyss, but when I started my second job at 25 I took out another card. I went to close the old one down until I realised that, actually, if I closed that, my years of owning a credit card would drop.
- Joint accounts with people you no longer know – when you join bank accounts, you are financially linking yourself and therefore, if they want to run a check on you and see a link, they can check on them as well. Imagine you're going on a date, and there is an option on the dating app to look at every previous relationship the person had. Would you look? Yes. So would I, and so would the bank. They want all the information.
  - The caveat here is joint bills. You can both be paying for the electricity together into a joint

bill, but it is not the same thing as a joint bank account.

- If you decide to close a joint account, it's a fairly straightforward process. First, make sure the account balance is zero by paying off any overdrafts or outstanding charges. Next, redirect any automatic payments, such as rent or bills, to another account. Most banks require both account holders to agree to close a joint account, so you'll need to visit a branch together or, with some banks, complete the process over the phone or online if both parties provide consent. Finally, follow up with the bank to confirm the account has been closed and request written confirmation for your records. This helps ensure that your credit file remains clean and unlinked from someone you're no longer financially tied to.

Soft and hard searches

Soft searches happen when companies want to take a quick peek at your credit history to check your eligibility for a card or loan. This type of search doesn't affect your credit score. It's more of a background check to see if you're worth pursuing. You'll be able to see soft searches on your credit report, but they won't be visible to lenders, so they don't impact your creditworthiness. Again, think of it like a dating app; they can look at your profile without committing to swiping right or left.

On the other hand, hard searches are done when you actually apply for credit. These searches leave a mark on your credit report and can affect your score. If you rack up too many hard searches in a short time frame, it can signal to lenders that you're desperate for credit, which can lower your score. So, when applying for credit, it's always good to space out those hard searches.

Section 75 protection:

One of the best perks of using a credit card, aside from building your credit score, is Section 75 protection. It's a law from the 1970s that offers you extra security when making purchases between £100 and £30,000. The protection doesn't depend on how much you spend on the card but on the purchase price of the item.

Section 75 means that the credit card company shares liability with the retailer if something goes wrong with your purchase, whether the product is faulty, doesn't arrive, or the company goes bust. In these cases, you can claim your money back from the credit card company. Let's say you're buying a new iPhone; I would always use my credit card for something that expensive, so I'm protected in case something goes wrong.

Just be aware, you need to ensure that you are paying the retailer directly, as there is no Section 75 protection if you use a third-party seller or payment platform, including PayPal or Buy Now, Pay Later options.

To make a claim under Section 75, all you need to do is contact your credit card provider, and many even allow you to do this directly through their app. It's a handy little safety net when using your card for bigger purchases.

What happens if something goes wrong and I don't pay it off in full?

I'm here to teach you all the right ways to handle finance and money, but we're human. We are not perfect, and therefore, when things go wrong, reading a book that tells you only what you *should* be doing can be really unhelpful. So let me prepare you for when things go wrong; if they have, that's absolutely fine. Let's talk through what actually happens.

First up: If you don't pay the minimum amount:

1. There can be late payment fees.
2. The unpaid amount will start incurring interest at that APR interest rate we talked about before.
3. If you had any promotional rates going on, like a 0 per cent balance transfer or cashback up to the first x amount of money, you may find this ends if you don't repay the minimum amount. This can often mean a breach of contract, and therefore you're out of the deal.

4. In the worst-case scenario, if you continue to miss your minimum payments, you may find yourself being moved on to debt collection.

Secondly, if you JUST pay the minimum amount and not the full amount:

1. You will start accruing interest on the amount that you have effectively borrowed, so that's the limit that you've used less the minimum amount you've paid.
2. You will have debt, and you will be prolonging this debt if you don't pay it off in full.
3. The minimum payment affects your credit utilisation, which is the percentage of your available credit that you're using. For example, if you have a £1,000 credit limit and you've used £500 but only pay £100, your balance will still be £400. This means you're already starting the next month with 40% of your credit limit utilised, leaving less room for spending and potentially impacting your credit score.

What happens if I can no longer repay?

If you have credit card debt, are paying interest, and can't afford to pay it off in full, you could look at balance transfer cards. A balance transfer card allows you to move the debt from your existing credit card to a new one, usually at a much lower interest rate or even o per cent. This means you'll still owe money, but the amount of interest you pay can significantly decrease, giving you a chance to pay off the debt more efficiently. You'll often hear about 'o per cent balance transfer cards' because, during an introductory period (often 12–24 months), no interest is charged on the transferred balance. Your goal here is to find the card with the lowest interest rate and a timeframe that gives you enough breathing room to clear that debt without racking up more charges.

But what happens if you don't repay your debt or fall behind? Debt doesn't just disappear. It stays on your credit file for six years, affecting your credit score and potentially making it harder for you to borrow in the future, whether it's for a loan, mortgage or even another credit card. Missed payments or default on your credit card can lead to higher interest rates, late payment fees and potentially legal action from your lender if things really spiral.

It's important not to ignore these problems. The longer debt goes unpaid, the worse the consequences, from mounting interest to possible defaults. Ignoring it won't make it disappear; it will only add stress and pressure.

If you ever feel like your debt is becoming unmanageable and you're struggling to keep up with payments, there are free resources that can help. Organisations like StepChange, a debt charity, offer free advice and support. They can help you understand your options, negotiate with creditors on your behalf, and guide you toward solutions like debt management plans (DMPs), individual voluntary arrangements (IVAs) or even bankruptcy if necessary. They're there to support you, whether that's over the phone or online, and help you take back control of your finances.

So, what exactly are these options? A DMP is an informal arrangement with creditors where you agree to pay back what you owe over a longer period, often with reduced payments to make it more manageable. This option can be useful if you just need a little breathing room to get back on your feet.

An IVA is a bit different and more formal. It's a legal agreement between you and your creditors, arranged through a licensed insolvency practitioner. With an IVA, you agree to make regular payments over a set time, typically five to six years. At the end of this period, any remaining debt may be written off. IVAs can be a helpful option if you owe multiple creditors and need a structured way to pay down what you owe without ongoing interest piling up. However, IVAs do appear on your credit report and can affect your credit for up to six years, so it's worth considering carefully with guidance from a professional.

Bankruptcy is the most serious option and isn't a decision to take lightly. Declaring bankruptcy can feel daunting, but in some cases, it's the reset button people need to clear overwhelming debt. Through bankruptcy, most of your debts are written off, giving you a fresh start. However, it also means that some of your assets, like your home or car, may need to be sold to cover what you owe, and it will stay on your credit report for six years, affecting your ability to borrow in the future. Debt charities can guide you through this process if it's necessary, ensuring you know what to expect and how to navigate the aftermath.

The key here is not to let fear silence you. It's easy to feel overwhelmed and think, *If I just ignore this, it will go away*. But facing the problem is always the best route. Reach out to organisations like StepChange before things get worse.

Student loans

Why do people go to university? Statistically, it's because those with a degree are likely to out-earn those without one over their lifetime. But there's more to the story than just that. Back in the late 1990s, former prime minister Tony Blair wanted to reduce unemployment, and one clever way to do that was to get more people into higher education; when you're in education, you're technically not counted as unemployed. This led to a massive push, convincing almost every 17-year-old that university was the only path to success.

While university can be a great way to build knowledge and skills, it's not always the golden ticket to financial success it's made out to be. Enter student loans, which are one of the most unusual types of debt you'll ever come across. Unlike a credit card, where monthly payments are fixed regardless of how much you earn, student loans in the UK work on a threshold system. You don't start paying anything back until you earn above a certain income level, which is very different from the US, where repayments start regardless of your salary.

Now, let's rewind a bit. There was a time when university was free. In fact, some people were even paid to go, thanks to grants and scholarships. But in 1998, things changed. Universities started charging around £1,000 a year for tuition. That eventually jumped to £3,000, which was frustrating but manageable. Then, after campaigning on a promise to abolish tuition fees, Nick Clegg, in coalition with David Cameron – in a move that angered an entire generation, including me – went on to triple them to £9,000 per year. Suddenly, the total cost for a three-year degree went from £9,000 to £27,000 in tuition alone. Thanks for that, Nick. My first year of university was 2012, which was when the new fees were introduced.

Today, tuition fees stand at £9,250 a year, and universities want them to rise with inflation. So, the big question becomes: if fees keep increasing, is a degree really worth it, and how do student loans really work in practice?

How do they work?

If you're planning to take out a student loan, here's how the system works. Before you head off to university, you'll apply for your student loan through the Student Loans Company (SLC). This loan is split into two parts: the tuition loan and the maintenance loan.

1. Tuition loan: This covers the cost of your actual tuition fees. Let's say your university charges the current maximum of £9,250 a year. The tuition loan will cover this entire amount, which gets paid directly to your university. You don't see a penny of it; it's all handled behind the scenes. The key thing to know is that this loan is *not* means-tested, meaning it doesn't matter how much your parents earn; everyone is eligible for the full tuition loan to cover the cost of their studies.

2. Maintenance loan: This is where things get a bit more personal. The maintenance loan is designed to cover your living costs, including rent, food, travel and books. However, this loan *is* means-tested, meaning the amount you can borrow depends on your household income. If your family earns above a certain threshold, you might only be eligible for the minimum maintenance loan, which is around £3,597 per year, paid out in three instalments.

On the other hand, if your household income is below that threshold, you could be eligible for the maximum maintenance loan, which is currently just above £13k: a higher amount that better covers the cost of living independently at university.

The tricky part? The gap between what the minimum loan offers and what you might actually need to live on can be significant. For many students, this means relying on family support, part-time work or other sources of income to make ends meet during their time at uni.

When to pay back

So, when does student loan repayment kick in, and how does it work? The good news is you don't have to start paying it back immediately after you finish university. Repayments begin in the April *after* you leave, so if you finish your studies in, say, May, you won't need to make any repayments until 11 months later, regardless of your salary throughout that time.

Once repayments do begin, your maintenance loan and tuition loan are bundled into one single loan. This combined loan will then be repaid based on your earnings, not as a flat monthly fee. The more you earn, the more you pay back, but until you hit a certain salary threshold, you won't pay anything at all (we'll break down those thresholds shortly).

One thing to keep in mind is that interest starts accumulating on your student loan *as soon as you begin university*. There was a time when interest didn't kick in until after you graduated, but those days are long gone. Why the change? People used to game the system, taking out loans, parking them in a high-interest savings account and collecting the interest for themselves, only to pay off the loan in full at the end of their degree. The Student Loans Company caught on to this and decided to charge interest from day one.

So, when you finish your degree, you're not just leaving with the original loan amount, say £40,000, but also the interest that's been racking up over the three or more years of study.

A common misconception is that student loans are like a 'graduate tax', but here's the thing: you'll be left with the debt whether you graduate or not. As long as you've taken out a student loan, you'll have to repay it, provided your earnings meet the repayment threshold. As someone who is still paying off their student loan, I always recommend that people take a step back and look at the big picture.

Now, the interest rates on these loans vary depending on the year you went to university, and they're usually linked to inflation. But when inflation skyrocketed to 11.1 per cent in November 2022, the government had to step in to prevent student loan interest from spiralling out of control. The interest rate is now capped at 7.5 per cent, which is still high but better than double digits.

How does the calculation work?

Here's how your student loan payments work, broken down by plan type. Each plan has specific thresholds, interest rates and repayment terms, depending on when you took out the loan and where you studied.

Plan 1 is generally for students who began university pre-2012. If you're on this plan, you start repaying 9 per cent of your income above the threshold of £24,990. This loan type will be cleared after 25 years. Interest is RPI or the BOE base rate plus 1 per cent, whichever is lower.

Plan 2 covers those who started after 2012, with a repayment threshold of £27,295. Above that, you'll pay back 9 per cent of your income, and the loan is wiped after 30 years. Interest is RPI plus up to 3 per cent, based on income.

Postgraduate loans for English and Welsh students pursuing postgrad or doctoral studies starting after 2016 have a threshold of £21,000, with repayments at 6 per cent above this amount. The specific loan wipe-out date or terms can vary.

Plan 4 applies to Scottish students and has distinct terms and limits, which may align with some English plans but could have variations based on the Scottish system.

Plan 5 for English students starting university after 2023 has a lower threshold of £25,000, with 9 per cent taken from any income above that amount, a 40-year term, and interest set at RPI only.

Understanding the repayment plan relevant to your loan is essential, as it affects how much you pay back each month and when your debt will be cleared.

What else is on offer?

There are other ways to fund university beyond student loans. Options like sponsorships, scholarships and bursaries can significantly reduce or even eliminate the costs. Let's break each one down.

Sponsorships can be an excellent way to fund your degree, with some companies covering tuition maintenance and providing summer work placements in exchange for you working with them post-graduation. These opportunities are often found in fields like engineering, finance, law and healthcare, where companies see a strong return on investment by training students from the start. To explore specific sponsorships, visit company careers web pages or consult with your university's career services, as they frequently partner with companies offering such programmes.

Scholarships are usually merit-based, meaning they're awarded based on your talent or achievements in areas like academics or sport. Scholarships can range from small financial boosts to full coverage of tuition or equipment costs for your studies or sport. They're a fantastic option if you excel in a particular field and can help ease the financial burden without any repayment requirements.

Bursaries are a fantastic form of support, especially

for students from lower-income households, as they provide additional financial aid throughout university without the need for repayment. Typically means-tested, they're awarded based on household income and can significantly help with living costs. To see what bursaries may be available, check your university's financial aid office, as many universities offer their own bursaries, or visit government and educational websites that list national and local options for eligible students.

Payday loans

Payday loans are often marketed as a quick and easy solution for short-term cash flow problems. You borrow a small amount of money, usually up to £1,000, and agree to repay it with interest by your next payday. It sounds straightforward, right? But like many things that seem too good to be true, payday loans come with some serious risks that you need to be aware of.

You apply for a payday loan online or at a storefront, and if approved, the money is usually deposited into your bank account within hours. In exchange, you agree to repay the loan in full, plus interest, on your next payday. This can feel like a lifeline when you're facing an emergency expense, such as an unexpected car repair or medical bill.

Here's where things get tricky. The interest rates on payday loans are astronomical compared to other forms of borrowing. We're talking about APRs that can soar by over 1,000 per cent. For example, you might borrow £200, but if you can't pay it back on time, fees and interest can quickly push that amount much higher than what you initially borrowed. (There is an FCA regulation that caps this now.)

One of the biggest dangers of payday loans is the debt cycle they can create. If you're unable to repay the loan on time, many payday lenders will offer to 'rollover' your loan into a new one, along with additional fees and interest. This can trap borrowers in a cycle of debt that's incredibly difficult to escape, as more of your paycheque goes toward paying off loans, leaving you with less money for essential expenses.

In recent years, regulators like the Financial Conduct Authority (FCA) have cracked down on payday lenders to ensure they act more responsibly. Caps have been placed on the total cost of the loans, including interest and fees, but the potential for financial damage is still there.

While payday loans feel like a quick fix in a crisis, they can lead to bigger problems. If you find yourself in a spiral, please seek out free debt advice from StepChange, but also contact the lender and explain the situation; it is possible to regain control.

BNPL

Buy now, pay later (BNPL), also known as deferred payment credit, has surged in popularity in recent years. This innovative payment method allows consumers to make purchases and defer payments over a period, typically in interest-free instalments. While it offers convenience and flexibility, it also poses significant risks, especially in an unregulated market.

The BNPL market has seen exponential growth, with one in six UK adults using these schemes. Popular providers like Klarna and Apple Pay Later have revolutionised the way people shop. These services make it easy for consumers to spread the cost of their purchases, whether it's for clothing, electronics or even food delivery.

The rise in instant gratification spending (remember we talked about doom spending in Chapter 2) has led to quick borrowing to buy items we can't afford right now.

How BNPL works

BNPL services allow customers to split their payments into three or more instalments. This can be particularly appealing for expensive items or during sales periods. For example:

- Pay instalments: A common option where the total purchase amount is divided into three equal parts, paid over three months.
- Extended payment plans: Some providers offer extended plans for larger purchases, spreading payments over several months.

How BNPL Providers Make Money

BNPL providers make their money primarily through commissions from retailers. When a customer uses a BNPL service, the provider pays the retailer upfront and then collects the payments from the customer over time. Retailers pay the BNPL provider a commission for this service, similar to the interchange fees paid to debit and credit card providers. They do this because they know that without the incentive to spread the cost, they would have lost you and the sale, so they owe these BNPL sites one for keeping you around.

While BNPL schemes can offer financial flexibility, they also come with potential pitfalls:

- Lack of regulation: According to a research note by the FCA, BNPL services are currently unregulated. This means there are fewer protections for consumers compared to traditional credit products.
- Credit searches: BNPL providers typically do not perform detailed credit searches. This can lead to consumers accumulating more debt than they can afford, as existing debts are not considered in the approval process.
- Impact on credit reports: Credit reference agencies like Experian now include BNPL

transactions in credit reports. However, this information has not yet been factored into credit scores, allowing time for analysis and system updates.

Risks and Considerations

1. Debt accumulation: Without detailed credit checks, users might accumulate BNPL debts on top of other existing financial obligations, leading to potential financial strain.
2. Impulse spending: The ease and convenience of BNPL can encourage impulse purchases, which may not always be financially prudent.
3. Late fees and penalties: Missing a payment can result in hefty late fees, adding to the overall cost of the purchase.

BNPL, in my opinion, is a particularly dangerous product, making something financial look easy and friendly to young and especially vulnerable people.

Spread the cost with zero risk; who wouldn't want that? But these systems can spiral and actually promote really bad spending habits where you live well outside your means. It's like the social media lifestyle aspirations we spoke about in Chapter 2; you don't need to use debt to feel complete.

The FCA is currently reviewing BNPL services

with an eye toward regulation. Future regulations could include:

- Stricter credit checks: Implementing more rigorous credit assessments to ensure consumers can afford the payments.
- Transparent terms and conditions: Requiring providers to clearly explain terms, fees and potential penalties.
- Consumer protections: Introducing protections similar to those for traditional credit products, such as dispute resolution mechanisms and interest rate caps.

BNPL schemes offer a convenient way to manage spending, but they come with significant risks. As these services continue to grow in popularity, it is crucial for consumers to understand the potential pitfalls and for regulatory bodies to ensure adequate protection. Being informed and cautious can help individuals make the most of BNPL while avoiding the debt trap.

How to clear your debt

When it comes to paying off debt, there are two main strategies people tend to use. Both start the same way by listing out all your debts, figuring out how much interest you're paying on each, and calculating how much you still owe. You'll begin by making the minimum payment on each debt, but here's where the two methods diverge.

The snowball method

This method taps into the 'reward' centre of your brain. Once you've covered the minimum payments, throw any extra money at the smallest debt. The idea is to knock out the smallest debt quickly, giving you a sense of accomplishment that propels you forward. Once that debt is cleared, you move on to the next smallest, and so on. The motivation from these small wins can be powerful.

The avalanche method

On the flip side, this method focuses on tackling the debts costing you the most. After making the minimum payments, focus on the debt with the highest interest rate. This approach saves you more money in the long run because it reduces the amount you're paying in interest each month. The downside is that it might take longer to clear the first debt, but the financial benefits make it worth the wait.

Typically, high-interest debts come from things like credit cards or payday loans. If you're grappling with these, you might also consider o per cent balance transfer cards as an option to stop interest from piling up while you work on paying them off. Just be cautious of any fees or conditions associated with these offers.

For larger debts, like mortgages or personal loans, keep an eye on early repayment fees. Some lenders penalise you for paying off loans too quickly, so always check the terms before making extra payments.

What happens if I can't pay my debts?

Debt can sometimes feel like a rollercoaster. At first, it may seem manageable, but before you know it, things can spiral out of control. This is where debt starts to affect not only your finances but also your mental health. If you find yourself in this situation, the most important thing to do is reach out for help sooner rather than later.

There are several non-profit organisations like Step-Change and Citizens Advice that offer free, independent advice. They're there to help without judgement and can guide you through your next steps, both financially and mentally. Sometimes, just talking to someone about your debt can be a huge relief.

I hope you never reach this point, but it's essential to understand all your options. Bankruptcy is a last resort that halts creditors from chasing you for repayment. It's a serious decision and should only be considered when all other avenues have been exhausted. Declaring bankruptcy will stop most debts, but it doesn't cover everything; for instance, your student loans will still need to be repaid once you're earning above the threshold.

While bankruptcy may provide immediate relief, it comes with long-term consequences, especially for your credit score and future borrowing ability. The good news? You can rebuild your credit over time. It's a slow process, but with patience and smart financial habits, you can get back on track.

THINGS YOU NEED TO REMEMBER:

- Understand the difference between good and bad debt. Borrowing for things like education or a home can be smart, while debt for short-term wants can become a burden if not managed well.

- Use credit cards responsibly by paying off the balance each month to avoid high-interest charges and build a good credit score.

- If debt feels overwhelming, don't hesitate to reach out to free, non-profit organisations like StepChange for support before things spiral out of control.

11. Spending Money

Together, we've gone through earning, saving and borrowing, but now it's time to tackle spending. How we spend can shape our financial well-being just as much as how we earn.

From understanding why your energy bills have skyrocketed to finding ways to make the most of your holiday budget without drowning in post-trip regret, we're going to break it all down. We'll also dive into something that's become all too common: scams. With more of our lives moving online, scammers are evolving, so it's vital to stay one step ahead to avoid falling into the traps.

By the end of this chapter, you'll feel more confident about managing the key areas of spending so you can enjoy the rewards of your hard work without the stress of overspending or falling into financial traps.

Energy prices

Energy bills are one of those predictable yet unpredictable expenses. You know it's coming, but how much? Well, that's the annoying part. Unlike broadband, energy prices are subject to price fluctuations.

Energy prices in the UK are primarily governed by two main factors: wholesale costs and the price cap set by Ofgem, the UK's energy regulator. The price cap limits what gas and electricity suppliers can charge you per unit of energy. It's designed to protect households from unfair price hikes and ensure energy companies aren't overcharging, but it doesn't cover everything. Your standing charge, the flat fee you pay just for being connected to the energy network, isn't included in this cap.

Energy prices are influenced by global events, like supply shortages, political tensions and extreme weather. When wholesale energy costs rise, energy suppliers have to pay more, and this can be passed on to you in your bills. This is where Ofgem's price cap comes in; it sets a maximum that energy companies can charge per unit of energy, limiting how much your bills can go up.

The price cap is reviewed every three months, so if wholesale prices increase, the cap may also rise, meaning your bills could go up, even though the cap is meant to protect you from extreme jumps.

How to keep your energy bills down

1. Turn off appliances on standby: Many devices use energy even when not in use; turning them off at the plug socket can save more than you think.

2. Check your appliances' efficiency: Ensure they're running as efficiently as possible. Older appliances can use more energy than newer, energy-efficient models. You'll find energy ratings on the labels of modern appliances.

3. Washing at low temperatures: Dropping your wash cycle temperature can save a surprising amount on energy bills without compromising cleanliness.

4. Switch to LED lights: They use up to 90 per cent less energy than traditional bulbs, making them a smart investment.

5. Monitor your usage: Smart meters are great for this; they provide real-time data and can help you track where your energy is going.

6. Be smart with your heating: Lowering your thermostat by just 1°C could reduce your heating bill by as much as 10 per cent.

7. Submit regular meter readings: If you don't have a smart meter, submit readings to avoid being overcharged based on estimated usage.

8. Shop around: Regularly review your energy provider and compare with others to ensure you get the best rate and service.

And finally, if you're on a fixed-rate tariff, remember that within 49 days of your contract ending, you can switch suppliers without facing early exit fees. A fixed-rate tariff means that the price you pay per unit of energy is locked in for a set period, usually one or two years, regardless of market fluctuations. This offers stability and protects you from price hikes during the term, but it also means you won't benefit if energy prices fall. When your contract's end date is approaching, it's a good time to shop around for a better deal, as you can switch without penalties and potentially secure a lower rate going forward.

Going on holiday

From yen to euros, dollars to rupees, the world uses a wide variety of currencies. Here in the UK, we use the pound sterling (I really hope by this point in the book you know that), but the moment you step off the plane, your hard-earned cash might need to change into something else to be useful. Understanding how foreign currencies work, and the most cost-effective ways to use them, can make a big difference in how much your holiday really costs.

Currency exchange rates fluctuate constantly, which means the value of your pound will change depending on when and where you exchange it. Keeping an eye on exchange rates before you travel can help you plan when to get the best value for your money. However, it's not just the exchange rate you need to consider; it's also the fees you might pay when converting your currency or spending abroad.

When travelling, the key is finding a card that works

best for you while keeping fees and extra costs to a minimum. A lot of people assume their regular bank card will do the job, but that can lead to unexpected charges.

Let's break down the options:

Credit cards

These can be a fantastic tool when spending abroad, especially those that offer no foreign transaction fees or offer rewards like air miles or cashback. One major bonus of using a credit card abroad is the extra layer of protection it gives you, especially when it comes to larger purchases. If something goes wrong, like a hotel refusing to refund you or a booking not being honoured, your credit card issuer can step in. This is because of the Section 75 protection we discussed in Chapter 10. As long as you spend between £100 and £30,000 on your card, your card provider shares responsibility with the seller if something goes wrong. It's like having a safety net for your money while travelling.

Debit cards

Your regular debit card might work abroad, but many will charge foreign transaction fees, usually around 2–3 per cent of every transaction. It might not sound like much, but those fees add up quickly, especially if you're using your card for small daily purchases like coffee or meals. Some UK banks do offer special travel accounts or debit cards designed for use abroad, so it's worth checking if your bank has a more travel-friendly option.

Prepaid travel cards

These are becoming increasingly popular. You load them up with a specific amount of foreign currency before you leave and then use them like a debit card while you're away. The advantage here is that you can lock in a good exchange rate before you go, helping you avoid any nasty surprises if rates suddenly change. Many pre-paid cards don't charge foreign transaction fees either, so they're worth considering.

Cash

It's always handy to have some local currency in cash when you travel, especially for small, on-the-go purchases like taxis, tips and street food. But don't rely on cash for everything. Carrying too much cash can be risky, and if it gets lost or stolen, there's no way to recover it. Plus, many places abroad accept cards even for small purchases, so it's better to keep your cash reserves for emergencies.

One tip I learned the hard way was that it's best to use a credit card when hiring a car abroad. Car rental companies love their security deposits, and using a credit card to book gives you more protection if something goes wrong. Many car rental companies will 'hold' a deposit on your credit card when you hire a vehicle, but if you use a debit card, this money gets frozen in your account, leaving you with less to spend during your holiday.

Credit cards also often come with some additional insurance benefits, which could save you from paying extra for the car rental company's pricey insurance options. Just make sure to check the fine print on your card before assuming you're fully covered.

How to avoid scams

As the technical world advances, so do the scams. We can go through chapters and chapters of how to build your wealth, how to make sure you're saving the right amount and budgeting well for your future, but if you're not protecting yourself against scams you could be at risk of losing the lot. I know that sounds dramatic but it can honestly be life changing and not in a good way.

The general rule is that if it seems too good to be true, it probably is.

AI scams

Scammers are becoming increasingly sophisticated with AI, allowing them to create ads that appear as though they're endorsed by specific people. Someone whose name (and face) shows up in countless fake ads is Martin Lewis, the trusted founder of moneysaving-expert.com. Fortunately, Lewis has a strict rule against doing any advertisements, so you can immediately dismiss any ad claiming he's involved. However, not everyone has such a clear policy, making it difficult to tell if you're seeing the real person or an AI-generated imposter.

But here's the challenge: not everyone has that flat 'no-ad' rule. Scammers can easily clone your favourite financial influencer's social media accounts, tweak the handle slightly and use AI to mimic their posts, videos and even their speech. I've had this happen to me, with fake accounts pretending to be me and then messaging followers, offering 'investment opportunities' that sound legitimate. The key rule here? If it's unsolicited, it's probably a scam. I never DM first, and neither will any reputable financial expert or institution.

Phone scams

A prevalent phone scam involving certain phone providers has been targeting customers with fake offers of rewards like an Apple Watch, iPad or headphones, supposedly as a thank-you for loyalty. The scam begins with a call from someone pretending to be from your phone provider, offering a gift. To proceed, they ask for a six-digit code that they have just sent you. In reality, the scammer is attempting to reset your account password, using that code to gain access.

Once they're in your account, they will set up a new contract in your name and order a phone. Although you might think receiving a new phone doesn't sound too bad, here's where the real scam unfolds. After you receive the device, they call back, apologising for sending the 'wrong item' and requesting you return it to them. They provide a mailing address, which is actually their own, not the phone provider. Once you return the device, you never hear from them again, leaving you with a new contract to pay off and no gift.

If you or someone you know receives such a call, it's crucial to act quickly. Contact your phone provider as soon as you sense something is off. Quick action can often prevent the fraudulent contract from being finalised. Remember, phone providers will never ask for a six-digit code over the phone. If you receive a call with this request, it's a clear red flag. Hang up immediately and call the phone provider directly to report the incident. By staying vigilant and informed about these tactics, you can protect yourself and others from falling victim to scams like this.

Keep up to date with scams by looking at Which? for scam alerts, Citizens Advice – Scams Action and even your bank, who should be keeping you up to date with any prevalent ones. As we know, they're ever changing, so you need to keep an eye out.

THINGS YOU NEED TO REMEMBER:

- Understand how Ofgem's energy price cap works to protect you from excessive energy costs and look for ways to make your home more energy-efficient to save on bills.

- Use credit cards wisely when travelling for added protection on purchases, like rental cars and big-ticket items, while avoiding unnecessary fees.

- Be cautious of AI scams and phone scams, especially those asking for personal details or codes. Always verify directly with your service provider before sharing any information.

12. Buying vs. Renting

When it comes to where we live, one of the biggest financial decisions we face is whether to rent or buy. It's a choice that stirs a lot of emotions and opinions. You've probably heard people say, 'Renting is just throwing money away,' while others will argue that buying a house ties you down and limits your freedom. Both perspectives have merit, but the real question is: what's best for you?

In this chapter, we're going to explore the ins and outs of both renting and buying, from how to save for a house deposit to understanding the actual home-buying process, and what happens after you've got those shiny new keys in hand. Whether you're just starting out or are ready to jump into homeownership, it's all about understanding what works best for your lifestyle, your goals and, of course, your wallet.

Renting

Financially, renting is a straightforward process. It's a contract between the property owner or landlord and you, the tenant. There should ALWAYS be a contract.

It will lay out all the financial details, such as your monthly rent, how much notice you need to give if you want to move out, and how much notice the landlord must give if they want the property back. It also covers things like who is responsible for maintenance and repairs. Spoiler alert: in most cases, that's the landlord's job.

The biggest perk of renting vs. buying is that, as the tenant, you're not on the hook for many of the big-ticket responsibilities that come with homeownership. Sure, you need to keep the place clean and avoid any intentional damage, but if the boiler breaks down or the roof starts leaking, it's not your problem. This means you're not shouldering the financial burden of surprise repairs or renovations, making it a more flexible option for many people.

The landscape of renting has changed dramatically over the last few decades. Back in 1995, just one in five families with children rented their home. Fast forward to today, and that number has doubled to two in five. Nearly one-third of people aged 35 to 45 in England live in rented accommodation now, compared to just one-tenth in 2000.

One major factor is the rise of the remote working lifestyle. More and more young people are able to chose how and where they work, and how often they need to be in the office, which can expand the areas people can buy and might mean people don't need to commit to one area for long periods of time.

In previous generations, owning a home was seen as

the ultimate financial milestone, a symbol of stability and wealth. Homes were being built in abundance, and there were plenty to go around. Now, with a competitive housing market and rising prices, many of us are being told, 'Lower your expectations' if you even want a shot at homeownership.

For some, that might be the goal. But for many others, renting offers a level of freedom and flexibility that fits better with their current lifestyle, and that's OK.

Buying a house

Let me start by saying that buying a house has been seen as a badge of honour for a long time, in the same way people are expected to have kids and sensible cars. But buying a house is not the only route to success, and it's not always the best investment for everyone.

There, I said it, but it is also not always a guarantee of a good investment.

Many people don't see the benefits. For starters, it can sometimes cost you money if you don't stay in the property for more than a few years. Also, if you love the remote lifestyle and prefer not to live anywhere for too long, tying yourself down to one house is just not ideal. Also, and probably the most important, there are some big downsides to options like 95 per cent mortgages for those with less money or a smaller deposit to get on the housing ladder – they can cost a fortune, so let's be honest when we're having this 'buying your first home' conversation, because financially it's a mammoth commitment.

I know I'm being miserable – I promise you I'm not in real life – but I really hate books and articles where the chapter 'Buying Your First Home' is all sunshine and rainbows about how amazing it is and how it is right for everyone. It is not. With the doom and gloom out of the way, if you *are* ready to buy a home, because it works for you, let's understand the finances behind it.

But how do you know when you're truly ready to buy a home? For me, the shift came when I realised I wanted a permanent base, a space I could make my own without needing a landlord's permission to make changes. I was ready for stability, and buying was a natural next step.

Saving for a house

The first step in buying a home is saving for a deposit. This is typically between 5 per cent and 20 per cent of the property value you want to purchase. The higher your deposit, the less you'll need to borrow, which not only reduces your loan size but also secures better interest rates and lowers your monthly repayments.

To put it into perspective, the average home price for a first-time buyer is around £288k, which means an average 20 per cent deposit of about £57k. It's no small feat! The average age of a first-time buyer is now 33, a number that's been steadily rising as housing prices outpace wage growth.

Lifetime ISAs

We've already met this gem in the savings chapter, but just a reminder: the lifetime ISA (LISA) is a savings account with tax-free benefits and a maximum contribution limit of £4,000 per tax year, per person. What makes the LISA particularly appealing for first-time buyers is that the government gives you a 25 per cent bonus on top of your contributions. So, if you max out your £4,000 yearly contribution, the government will add an extra £1,000!

If there are two of you, you can use two LISAs when buying a first home, but just be aware you both have to be first-time buyers, and the property must be valued at £450k or less.

Your contributions each year are increased by 25 per cent as a contribution from the government BUT if you do not use it for your first home there are sadly only two options: take the money out with a 25 per cent hit on everything, the money they gave you and your own money; or leave it there until you turn 60.

Help-to-buy ISA

Help-to-buy ISAs were the predecessors of the LISA, and while you can't open one anymore, if you already have one, you can still use it. The mechanics are similar to the LISA in that your contributions get topped up by 25 per cent from the government, but there are a few key differences:

- The maximum value of the property you can buy using this ISA is £250,000 (or £450,000 in London).
- Your maximum contributions are lower, capped at £2,400 a year (£3,400 in the first year).

If you have a help-to-buy ISA, you might as well take advantage of the bonus while it's still available, but for new savers, the LISA is the only one on offer now to you. You can only receive the government bonus on one or the other, not both of these.

There was also a help-to-buy equity loan scheme where you could borrow up to 20 per cent of the property value (40 per cent in London) from the government as part of your deposit. Although this has now been scrapped, there's nothing to say it couldn't be brought back to stimulate house purchases.

Shared ownership

Shared ownership is another government scheme designed to make buying a home more accessible. With this option, you buy a percentage of the property (usually between 25 per cent and 75 per cent) and pay rent on the rest. Over time, you can 'staircase' by buying more shares of the property, gradually increasing your owner-ship until you own 100 per cent.

Shared ownership can be a good option if you're struggling to save for a full deposit, as the deposit is based only on the share of the property you're buying. However, keep in mind that you'll still need to pay rent on the portion you don't own, and there may be restrictions on selling the property, such as giving first refusal to the housing association.

BOMAD

BOMAD is the acronym of all acronyms, standing for the Bank of Mum and Dad. It turns out they are the ninth largest lender when it comes to first-time buyers, so we can't talk about first homes without mentioning them. The Bank of Gran and Grandad (BOGAG) is often included in this network, though it doesn't have quite the same ring to it.

While BOMAD can be a lifeline, these conversations can be emotionally charged. Money is a sensitive topic, especially when it involves family, and it's important to navigate these discussions carefully. One of the first things to establish is clarity: is this money a gift or a loan? This distinction is crucial, as it can affect everything from your relationship dynamics to inheritance tax planning. Bringing in a solicitor to outline clear terms might feel overly formal, but it can help avoid confusion or misunderstandings later.

Talking about money can be awkward, but setting the right tone helps. Start by acknowledging the discomfort: 'I know money can be tricky to discuss, but I'd love to explore this together.' Be honest about your position: 'I'm looking at buying a home and wondered if it's something we could work on together. I want this to feel right for everyone.' Clarify expectations: 'Would this be a loan I'd repay, or a gift? I'd like us to be clear upfront.' Finally, address the bigger picture: 'How might this impact your other financial goals, like retirement?' Approach the topic with empathy, listen to their concerns, and pause if emotions run high. The goal is to collaborate and ensure any support benefits everyone.

The actual home-buying process

Buying a house is exciting but also packed with fees and legal hurdles. It's not just about finding your dream home; you'll need to deal with lawyers, estate agents, banks and tax obligations along the way. Here's what you need to know to get through the process without too many surprises.

First things first, you'll need a solicitor or conveyancer to handle all the legal paperwork. This person will become a big part of your life for a few months, and trust me; you want someone you're comfortable calling, emailing and pestering because you'll be doing that a lot – a LOT. If you get a bad vibe or feel awkward reaching out to them, walk away and find someone else.

During my own flat purchase, I was on the phone with my solicitor more than some of my friends. I knew his girlfriend's name, his coffee order, and even that he liked tennis because I was in his office so often, trying to push things through. You're going to be in a mini-war together, so pick someone you feel good about going into battle with; for instance, we entered into a share-of-freehold agreement, and it came with trying to communicate with the other freeholder, who happened to live in Australia.

Estate agent fees, thankfully, aren't something you need to worry about as a buyer – that's on the seller. However, it's worth remembering that the estate agent technically works for the seller. Their job is to get the highest price for the property, which boosts their commission, so they aren't always on your side, no matter how helpful they may seem.

When you get a mortgage, the bank will likely send someone to value the property, and this isn't always free. You might end up paying for this valuation, so be aware of the small fees that can start to add up. You will also want the completion of a survey. A survey isn't just a box-ticking exercise; it's there to protect you as much as the valuation does for the bank. The valuation ensures the property is worth what you're paying for it, giving the lender confidence that their loan is secure. But the survey is designed to identify any hidden damages or faults in the property that could end up costing you significantly down the line.

Now let's talk about the big fee, the mortgage. We left that out of the borrowing money chapter so we could talk about it here.

A mortgage is typically calculated as around **4.5 times your salary**, although this has varied over the years. For example, if you earn £30,000 a year, you could potentially borrow around £135,000.

However, there are things to consider because it's not always worked out on your gross income:

- Student loans do come into play; they can reduce your available income.
- Big recurring expenses, like big monthly bills.
- Credit scores impact the rate at which the lender is willing to lend out.

When it comes to finding the right mortgage lender, you can go straight to the high street banks you know or even bring in a mortgage broker who can navigate your options based on your specific scenario.

Then think about the type of mortgage you're after. You could have a fixed rate for two, three or five years, sometimes more, where your payment won't change. Alternatively, there are variable mortgages, which could track things like the Bank of England base rate, rising and falling depending on their decisions.

Stamp duty land tax (SDLT)

You can't talk about buying houses without talking about stamp duty land tax. It's a hefty tax and it can be really difficult to work out why we're actually paying it.

It's like income tax, in that it is done in thresholds.

If your house falls under a certain threshold as a first-time buyer, you are exempt from paying SDLT, but if it goes over you pay a tax. However, there's a weird added layer of rules depending on whether or not you're a first-time buyer. If you aren't, and if this an additional property on top of one you already own, you can expect to pay an additional 5% on top of your SDLT rates.

This is a tax on the purchase; it's not a tax on the seller, so it does sometimes put people off from moving around as often as they might like.

What to think about when you have the keys

I was once advised that you need to plan to spend at least £500 the day you walk through the door. As some-one that bought a flat that was falling apart at the seams I saw that coming. But I also know people who have bought new builds, that ended up spending the same amount because there are so many little things that we forget need to happen.

Take curtains – who knew curtains weren't just built into houses? Turns out everyone except first-time buyers. It almost feels like a tradition that you aren't allowed a decent night's sleep for your first few weeks because curtains are a luxury for the adults, and you're not one of those until quite a few weeks after buying the property.

THINGS YOU NEED TO REMEMBER:

- Buying a home isn't always the best financial move and doesn't guarantee a profitable investment. Consider your lifestyle, commitment level and financial stability before diving in; homeownership comes with substantial long-term responsibilities.

- Your mortgage choice and the related fees (like stamp duty and valuation fees) can significantly affect your budget. Fixed-rate mortgages provide stable payments, while variable rates fluctuate, so choose according to your risk tolerance and budget flexibility.

- The expenses don't stop once you've paid the deposit and mortgage.

PART FIVE

Building your Wealth

We're almost there; we've covered the essentials, understanding money, what your money is all about and managing your money. It's time to shift to building wealth; looking forward and focusing on how to grow your money and secure your financial future.

We'll dive into three key chapters, each with its own unique approach to wealth-building. First, we'll explore the world of investing, what it means, how to get started and how to make your money work for you over time. From stocks to bonds to real estate, this chapter will give you a solid foundation in how to build long-term financial growth.

Next up is pensions, the ultimate long game in personal finance. Whether you're already contributing or just getting started, understanding how to maximise your pension is crucial for securing a comfortable retirement. We'll break down the different types of pensions, what you need to consider, and how to make sure you're on track.

Finally, we'll explore other wealth-building ideas, such as investing in yourself. From learning new skills to starting a side hustle, this chapter is about thinking beyond traditional investments and recognising that wealth isn't just about money, it's also about personal growth and opportunities.

13. Investing

So, talk to me. Are you investing? There are quite a few groups when it comes to investing. You've got the people who have never invested who will say, 'I don't know enough to invest.' They'll leave it at that, and there won't be any more conversations. Then, at the other end, there's the 'buy low, sell high' gang, swapping stories about their latest stock trades like they're in *The Wolf of Wall Street*.

Here's the thing: investing is *very* different from saving. That's why I didn't put the savings chapter into the 'Building your Wealth' part of this book. Saving doesn't build wealth; investing in its different forms does. Savings accounts keep your money safe, sure, but if you want it to grow and actually work for you, investing is the way to go.

My goal with this chapter? To show you that you don't need a ton of money or insider knowledge to start investing. In fact, starting small is often best for your education. We'll break down the jargon and uncover why bulls and bears don't have anything to do with animals but rather market changes. Investing has long felt like an elite, exclusive club, but we're not about that anymore. It's time to make it accessible and doable for *you*. So, let's get stuck in and see how you can start building your wealth, one smart move at a time.

What is investing?

Investing is buying products in the hope that they'll be worth more in the future than you're paying for them today.

This spans a whole host of wealth-building opportunities, including stocks, bonds, REITs (real estate investment trusts) and more (all of which I'll discuss in detail in just a bit), but it's about building money for a point in time.

Investing doesn't always feel natural as a form of personal finance; it feels the riskiest and the most elitist. Many of us weren't invited to sit at that table. This can often be due to loss aversion. This is a concept from behavioural economics that explains how we are more sensitive to loss than gains.

Take £20. Let's say you drop a £20 note on your way to work. The disappointment you feel tends to be much more intense than the excitement you would feel if you found £20 in the pocket of a pair of old jeans you never wear. This bias can be a huge reason people avoid the stock market and investing in general. We hear it's risky, and we are aware when the news starts with 'the stock market is down'. But it's just about habits and understanding. I want to help you get past this.

An economist called John Maynard Keynes created a concept called 'animal spirits', which helps explain why investing can feel risky. He described how emotions like confidence, fear, optimism and pessim-ism often drive people's economic decisions, leading to irrational or unpredictable behaviour in financial mar-kets. When people are confident, they invest and spend more, boosting the economy. But when uncertainty or fear sets in, even good investment opportunities can be ignored, causing economic activity to slow down. This highlights that economic decisions aren't always purely logical; they're deeply influenced by emotions, which is why investing can feel intimidating.

When it comes to buying investments, the first term to understand is 'the market', which is where buyers and sellers come together to trade assets like stocks, bonds and commodities. It's essentially a system that allows people to buy ownership in companies, lend money through bonds and invest in other assets like real estate. The prices of these assets fluctuate based on supply and demand, investor sentiment and broader economic factors. When you invest in the market, you're partici-pating in this dynamic system, where values can rise or fall depending on how the overall economy or specific industries perform.

The market is volatile; it goes up and down like a yo-yo. However, what also tends to happen with market volatility is media coverage. The media will declare that the market is down 1,000 points or that the Japanese stock market has dropped 12 per cent, and the ripple effect can feel like all your money invested is about to fall off a cliff. These are 'panic days'.

What do 'panic days' look like, and how do you prepare?

The market for equities (stocks and shares), bonds, currency, commodities and everything in between has days where the price rises and days when the price falls. External factors will impact this. For instance, at the beginning of August 2024, a jobs report came out for the US that stated that in July, 114k jobs had been created; that seems good, right? Well, it wasn't if you compared it to the forecast of 185k. It actually seemed like a loss and those who invested in the US believed this meant the US was headed for recession.

A recession is two consecutive quarterly drops in economic growth, and the US hadn't even hit one, but almost instantly the market started to react and sell off shares. At the time, one of the most respected investors in the world, Warren Buffett's investment company, Berkshire Hathaway, sold off over half of its shares in Apple. It coincided with the earnings report that, while showing increased revenue, wasn't clearly showing the signs Berkshire Hathaway wanted to see.

Following this drop of Apple stock by Buffett and jobs coming in lower than expected, the US sneezed, and the world seemed to catch a cold; as this all happened on Friday, Monday saw the Japanese stock market drop 12 per cent in a day – a day! Then the UK saw a 2 per cent drop; there were hits everywhere. Within a day, though, things started to change. Japan rose by

10 per cent the following day, and things started to ease, but it's easy to see how a few pieces of data can have an instant and chaotic effect on the market.

A common phrase used for market conditions is bull and bear; once I tell you what I'm about to tell you, you will find it impossible to forget this; the two words refer to how the animals attack.

The bull part refers to when stock prices rise, representing high investor confidence and an upward stock price trajectory. You might also hear this referred to as a bullish market or a bull market. This is because when bulls come together and fight, their horns collide, and when their horns collide, they rise, raising prices.

Now, the bear part is the opposite. A bear market refers to stock prices falling due to low investor confidence and a general downward trajectory of the stock price. This is because when bears fight, their paws go down.

Ridiculous, isn't it? I felt like I needed to explain bull and bear when I started talking about investing really early on to give everyone the confidence that if investing and the jargon around it is this ridiculous, then how hard can the rest be?

When prices are down in the market, and you are just a regular investor – meaning you aren't engaging in day trading, which involves buying and selling stocks or assets within a single trading day to take advantage of short-term price movements – it can be easy to check your investment and say, 'I've lost money', but you haven't in the long term. You only realise the loss if you sell when it's down. This phrase will come back time and time again in this chapter, but it's important to remember. It is time in the market, not timing the market. No one knows the highest point a stock will reach or the lowest, and that is why when you invest, it is for the long term: ride the waves.

Types of investments

Stocks and shares

What's the difference between a stock and a share? Really, it's nothing. Some will say it comes down to the specifics. Let's say you have stock in a tech company as a general term, whereas if you have 50 shares of Alphabet, that's a more specific metric, but the two are the same: having a stock in Tesla and a share in Tesla is the same thing.

You can pick individual stocks; this is about owning a piece of a specific company you've chosen. Suppose you just go out in search of picking stocks in companies. In that case, you might find your portfolio of investments quite volatile; putting all your money into stocks, also known as equities, is putting all your eggs in one basket.

It can be interesting to have a few individual stocks in industries you're interested in, and it keeps you coming back to check on how they're doing. For instance, I invested a very small amount in Ferrari. I'm a huge fan of Formula 1, and I follow it quite closely. I found it so interesting to see the change in the stock price when the drivers changed. When Lewis Hamilton replaced Carlos Sainz, the stock price of Ferrari shot up, and it was a very easy reflection of how the world interacted with the market. If I'd bought the shares the day before the announcement and sold them the day after, I would have made a gain.

Speaking of my shares in Ferrari, you can have whole shares, where you own one whole piece of the pie, or you can have what's known as fractional shares, where the shares are split into fractions. This makes investing so much more accessible for many as whole shares in businesses can cost thousands, but having just £20 in your account means you can still afford a fraction of a whole share.

If you want to spread your risk in the stocks and shares investment world, you're going to want to understand funds, which I will go into below.

When it comes to the split of stocks in your portfolio, there is the 100 Rule, which helps you figure out how much of your portfolio should be in equities (stocks and shares) based on your age. The rule is simple: subtract your age from 100. If you're 25, the rule suggests putting 75 per cent of your investment portfolio in stocks and the rest in lower-risk assets like bonds. The idea here is that the younger you are, the more risk you can afford to take, as you have more time to recover from any losses. Sadly, I'll be putting less than 75 per cent into my investment portfolio.

Share prices fluctuate. The market can be volatile, and this can be caused by earnings reports showing weaker business earnings than expected or even when companies decide to repurchase shares. Earnings reports are issued quarterly by publicly traded companies to disclose their financial performance, including metrics such as revenue, profit and expenses. These reports are prepared and released by the companies themselves, often accompanied by statements from their leadership teams to provide insights into the results and outlook.

Earnings reports pay attention to their quarterly earnings reports. These reports contain important data that can affect the stock price, such as profit, revenue and projections. It's a good idea to review these reports to understand how your investment is performing.

Repurchasing shares reduces their circulation and makes the remaining shares more valuable. This signals that the company is doing right by its shareholders and is confident in its growth. This happens for many reasons; another could be that it thinks its shares are undervalued and knows what it has planned for growth.

A company might do this instead of paying a dividend to be tax efficient. With a dividend, the income to the shareholder is taxed (unless it's in an ISA), whereas the increased value of a share is only taxable when it's sold.

When evaluating your investment, you want to look at both the numbers (quantitative) and the bigger picture (qualitative). Quantitative data includes earnings, revenue and growth rates, while qualitative data considers factors like the company's reputation, management quality and industry trends. Combining both helps you to make a more informed decision; it is worth checking when you go to invest what sort of business you want to associate yourself with, and while sometimes it's simple – the ones that are going to give me good returns – the qualitative side can complicate the decision with factors such as whether a company cares about its employees or the environment.

How do you make money in stocks and shares?

There are two ways you make money in the stock market: dividends and capital gains.

Dividends are where companies release a certain amount of their profits to their shareholders; they don't do this out of the goodness of their hearts. They do this because you'll often find their c-suite are also investors and paying them out dividends as income comes at a lower tax rate than income. If they release a dividend to one shareholder, they have to release it to all shareholders.

If you sell your share for more than you paid for it, this is known as a capital gain. This is income earned on your share. If this is in a stocks and shares ISA, you wouldn't have to pay tax; however, if it's in a general investment account, you may have a tax liability.

Funds

This is when you bring various elements together to create a fund; think of it like shopping in the 'investment' supermarket, and instead of just going to the stocks and shares aisle you can also head down the bonds and crypto aisles, putting different assets into one basket.

Funds can also track indexes. Index funds are a basket of investments that replicate the companies in a certain index. For example, the FTSE 100 index fund is a basket of the top 100 companies. The S&P 500 represents the top 500 US companies. Or more recent indexes such as the Magnificent Seven, which tracks the top seven biggest tech companies. Index funds are usually considered good long-term investments because they're diversified; you're investing in a fund that has lots of investments within it.

Also, when one company drops out of the top 500, the index will adjust itself: another great example of making your money work for you without you having to do anything.

ETFs stands for exchange-traded funds. With an ETF, you invest by buying a number of shares of that fund, kind of like you do with stocks. Since most ETFs track the performance of a certain index, like the S&P 500, or an asset, sector, tech or regional market, like the US, they don't need a human to monitor them.

They trade all day, just like a stock, with prices fluctuating constantly.

Mutual funds, on the other hand, are priced once daily as someone behind a desk picks and chooses the funds. That person is trying to beat the market, and there is a minimum buy-in which will be thousands, as opposed to buying fractions of ETFs.

Bonds, REITs and commodities

Bonds are the safest investment we will run through in this chapter. This is where you lend money to the government, big banks and even big companies. You know the return you'll get in the long term up front. One-year, five-year and even ten-year bonds are common; when they expire, you get your money back or you can transfer it into new ones. And you can get bought out midway. These bonds give you a known return in the future that's set, unlike the stock market, and by their nature, you know you'll get your initial investment back with interest.

Real estate investment trusts are a type of investment that allows you to invest in property without actually having to buy or manage buildings yourself. In the UK, REITs are companies that own and operate income-generating real estate, such as offices, shopping centres, hotels and even residential buildings. These companies rent out the properties they own and then distribute the rental income to investors in the form of dividends.

By law, REITs must distribute at least 90 per cent of their rental income to shareholders. So, as an investor, you'll regularly receive a portion of the profits from the properties the REIT owns. REITs are traded on the stock market, which means you can easily buy and sell shares whenever you want. The value of REIT shares can go up or down, depending on how the property market is performing, but you also benefit from the regular income, which makes REITs an appealing option for long-term investors.

Commodities, gold, diamonds and even wheat are physical goods that you can trade in the market. Unlike stocks, which represent company ownership, commodities are products that people use, from metals like gold and silver to energy sources like oil and natural gas and agricultural goods like coffee, wheat and sugar. Commodities are essential for many industries, and global events, weather and supply-demand changes can influence their prices.

While commodities can be a good way to diversify, they are also known for their volatility, meaning prices can go up or down quickly and unpredictably. For example, the price of oil can fluctuate based on geopolitical events or changes in supply. Similarly, agricultural commodities like wheat or coffee can be affected by weather conditions, which makes them unpredictable.

How do you make money in bonds, REITs and commodities?

With bonds, you know your term time and the return you'll get once that time has passed. This means a bond with a 5 per cent return in five years' time will pay you 5 per cent of your money at the end of five years, which is stable for many people. The returns can be lower because the risk is lower.

By investing in REITs, you can benefit from both ongoing income through dividends and potential growth in the value of your shares.

Commodities are similar to stocks and shares, and you're hoping the value of the commodity will rise over time. There is something called futures contracts where you can bet on the price of something going up or down, and for those, you can even earn money betting the value of the commodities will drop.

Cryptocurrency and NFTs

Cryptocurrency has become a bit of a buzzword, mainly because it challenges our traditional understanding of money. It doesn't need to be secured by a central bank like the Bank of England, which shakes up the financial system as we know it. But let's break it down: what is cryptocurrency, and why is everyone talking about it?

At its core, cryptocurrency is a digital or virtual form of money stored and exchanged on something called a blockchain. A blockchain is essentially a digital ledger that records transactions securely across many computers. Unlike traditional currencies, where banks oversee and process payments, cryptocurrencies such as Bitcoin operate on a decentralised system, meaning no central authority (like a bank) is in charge. It's peer-to-peer, allowing people to send money directly to each other without needing a middleman.

But here's the thing: cryptocurrencies are highly speculative. No real-world asset or intrinsic value is backing them. Bitcoin and Ethereum are two of the big names in this space, but technically, anyone can create their own cryptocurrency. This is both exciting and risky. Because it's unregulated, the price of cryptocurrencies can swing wildly. One day, you could see massive gains; the next, your investment could drop significantly in value. And while people do refer to crypto as 'currency,' most people don't actually spend it like regular money. Instead, it's mostly held as an asset, something people hope will increase in value over time.

Now, if you're thinking of jumping into the crypto game, here's something to remember: it's not the same as investing in stocks or bonds. Unlike those assets, cryptocurrencies don't offer tax breaks, and they aren't tied to real-world value in the same way. Plus, because of the volatility, they're not reliable as a store of value. Think about it: if your Bitcoin is worth £80,000 one day and £10,000 the next, would you really want to use that to buy your weekly groceries?

While crypto is exciting, and many are drawn to it because it feels like the next big thing, be cautious. If your investment strategy is purely based on hype from social media or fear of missing out, you're setting yourself up for a rough ride. The lack of regulation means that if things go wrong, there's no safety net. There's also no guarantee that what you invest will increase in value; people have lost significant sums in the crypto market.

That said, the rise of cryptocurrency has forced governments and central banks to rethink how we view money. It has introduced the idea of digital currencies that don't need to exist in physical form. This is where concepts like central bank digital currencies (CBDCs) come into play. These are digital versions of a country's traditional currency, issued and regulated by the central bank. For example, in the UK, there's been talk of a digital pound. CBDCs would be regulated, unlike cryptocurrencies, giving them a more stable value.

So, while crypto may not be replacing your bank account anytime soon, it's certainly influencing the future of money in ways we never thought possible. But as with any investment, approach it with caution, do your research and don't be swayed by the hype.

Ethical investing

Like many industries, we are becoming more aware of the ethics and morals behind our decisions. Just as we understand that excessive use of fossil fuels contributes to climate change, we're also waking up to the idea that our money has real power in the investing world, what we call 'share power'.

Share power refers to the influence you hold as a shareholder in a company. When you own shares, you own a piece of that company, and with that comes a voice. Much like the directors who sit on the board, you can have a say in how the business is run. In her excellent book *Share Power*, Merryn Somerset Webb emphasises the importance of not simply selling off shares in companies we view as 'bad'. Instead, by holding on to them, we maintain the ability to push for the changes these companies promise, ensuring they stay accountable to their shareholders.

When it comes to investing, it's not just about making money – it's about putting your money where your values are. It's about investing in companies and industries that align with your interests, morals and insight. And part of that is doing your research to ensure these businesses are doing right by the planet, their employees and their finances.

We also can't ignore the religious aspects of investing. Certain faiths, like Islam, have specific guidelines that practising investors must follow under the principles of their religion. I'm not an expert in this area, but it's important to recognise that ethical and moral investing can take many forms. For some, it includes adhering to these religious requirements.

How to invest

There are two options for setting up an investment account (not including pensions): a general investment account or a stocks and shares ISA.

A general investment account (GIA) is sort of like a current account for your investments; think of it like a basket where you can buy commodities, stocks, bonds – whatever you like – and hold them in that account. Most GIAs won't charge a fee, but there may be fees when you buy or sell the assets in the portfolio.

A stocks and shares ISA, on the other hand, may have a monthly fee; however, as apps and investment companies become more competitive, these fees are being competed away.

The biggest difference is the tax liability; if your investment is in an S&S ISA, there is no tax to pay; however, in a GIA, there could be tax liabilities, but I'll cover that in the last section.

Taking that first step into investing can feel intimidating, but starting small is a great way to build confidence over time. The key is to begin with what you can afford. You don't need a large sum to get started, as many platforms allow you to invest with as little as £1 or £20. The goal here is to set a budget based on what you can comfortably invest, knowing that this money will be tied up for the long term.

If you're cautious about risk, consider beginning with

lower-risk investments like index funds or ETFs (which we saw earlier). These give you broad exposure to a range of companies and help spread out the risk, making it a safer option for beginners. It's a good way to start without needing to dive into individual companies right away.

To make things even easier, many platforms allow you to automate your investments. This means you can set up regular contributions, allowing you to invest small amounts consistently without having to worry about timing the market. It's a simple yet powerful way to build wealth over time, and you won't have to stress about making decisions every month.

Once your portfolio is up and running, you sit back. We aren't day trading; we're building wealth, and building takes time. You might find yourself in the first few weeks of investing jumping onto the app and taking a quick scan at whether it's risen or fallen and why, but over time, it's best to leave it be.

There's a process called 'lifestyling' commonly spoken about around pensions, which, as we know, are investments. The investment will affect your lifestyle throughout your life and adjust your risk appetite depending on how close you are to retirement. The same goes for all investments; if your investments are already in target-date or lifestyle funds, this will happen automatically, but if you're choosing your portfolio stock by stock, you might find yourself needing to adjust yearly as your goals and life change.

Another investment method is called 'Pound cost averaging' a strategy that involves regularly investing a fixed amount of money into the market, regardless of whether prices are rising or falling. This approach allows you to buy more units when prices are low and fewer units when prices are high, smoothing out the average cost of your investments over time. By staying consistent, it takes the pressure off trying to time the market perfectly and helps reduce the impact of volatility. It's like drip-feeding your investments, ensuring you're always participating in the market rather than waiting for the 'perfect' moment, which rarely exists.

If I had to sum up this chapter in one word, it would be time. Time in the market is one of the most critical factors when it comes to building wealth through investing; this is about long-term growth.

Studies show that if you leave your investment in an index fund for just one year, there's a 25 per cent chance you might lose money. But over five to ten years, that chance drops significantly, and ultimately becomes negligible. The key is to stay invested and avoid reacting emotionally to short-term market dips. Remember, investing is a marathon, not a sprint.

So, resist the temptation if you're thinking about pulling out of the market after just a few weeks because your portfolio is down. You've got to give it time to grow.

Taxes

It might feel strange to end a chapter on investing by talking about tax, but it's an essential part of the process. Taxes are often the last thing we think about when we're excited about growing our wealth, but they can have a significant impact on your returns. Understanding the tax implications of your investments is crucial to maximising what you keep.

There's a dividend tax for investments like stocks, shares and REITs. If you own shares in a company and that company pays dividends (a share of its profits), you might have to pay tax on those dividends. Luckily, there's an annual dividend allowance of £500 that lets you earn a certain amount of dividend income tax-free. For anything over that allowance, the tax rate you pay will depend on your income tax band. So, while dividends can provide a great income stream, don't forget that the taxman takes a cut once you surpass the allowance.

And for any gains made on your investments, such as commodities, there is capital gains tax: If you sell your stocks or shares for more than you paid for them, the profit you make is known as a capital gain. Like with dividends, there's an annual allowance for capital gains of £3k, meaning you can make a certain amount of profit each year before you owe any tax. However, if your gains exceed the allowance, you'll pay capital gains tax, which varies depending on your overall income and the type of asset you're selling. As discussed earlier in the tax chapter, different assets have different tax rates, and it's important to factor this into your investment strategy.

As we covered above, if you invest within a stocks and shares ISA, you won't have to pay either dividend tax or capital gains tax on any profits you make. The tax-free benefits of an ISA make it a powerful tool for long-term investing, allowing your money to grow without the worry of tax liabilities and if you weren't using a S&S ISA and made investment income you would have to declare your investment income, you'd do this through self-assessments.

So, while taxes may not be the most exciting part of investing, understanding how they apply to your investments is key to keeping more of your hard-earned returns. And by making smart use of tax-efficient accounts like ISAs, you can significantly reduce your tax liability and give your investments more room to grow.

THINGS YOU NEED TO REMEMBER:

- Unlike saving, investing allows your money to grow by putting it to work in assets like stocks, bonds or funds. It carries more risk but offers higher potential rewards.

- Spread your money across different types of investments, such as stocks, funds, REITs and bonds, to help manage risk. Don't put all your eggs in one basket!

- Whether you're investing in stocks, funds or even cryptocurrencies, starting with what you can afford and using strategies like pound cost averaging can help you grow your wealth without feeling overwhelmed.

14. Pensions

Your pension is likely to be one of the biggest pots you'll build up over your lifetime, yet it's often the least talked about. While many young people today are rethinking the traditional idea of retirement, imagining a life where work and freedom blend more fluidly, pensions still play a crucial role in securing financial stability for your future. Whether you plan to retire early or not at all, understanding how pensions work is essential to making sure you have the flexibility to make choices down the line.

In this chapter, we'll break down everything you need to know about pensions. From the basics of the state pension to workplace schemes, private pensions and SIPP (self-invested personal pension) accounts. We'll also cover how to access your pension funds when the time comes. Whether you're just starting out or already well into your career, this chapter will help you understand how to build and protect your pension so your future self can thank you.

The state pension

The state pension is often viewed as a guarantee, but it's actually a benefit, meaning the government has the power to adjust or change it as it sees fit. In fact, there have already been discussions about introducing means testing for the state pension in the future, which could further change how it works.

So, what do you get? The full weekly new state pension currently sits at around £230. The roots of the state pension can be traced all the way back to the Old Age Pension Act of 1908, which was designed to support men returning from war who couldn't return to work. Fast forward to today, and the state pension is now available to anyone who meets the eligibility criteria.

To qualify for any of the new state pensions, you need at least ten years of national insurance contributions; you need 35 full years to get the maximum amount.

The landscape has shifted dramatically over time. Back in the 1960s, around 31 per cent of men didn't live to see pension age, and those who did lived on average for just 12.5 years after starting to claim it. Today, people are living around 23 years beyond the state pension age, making it more expensive to sustain as we have the largest population of pensioners in history.

Many pensioners often say, 'I've paid into this system all my life; I'm entitled to it,' but that's not exactly how it works. The government funds pensions from current taxpayers, and adjustments can be made depending on economic and political factors.

Pensioners also tend to assume that their state pension will increase every year. While this has been true in recent years thanks to something called the triple lock agreement, it's not a guarantee set in stone. The triple lock ensures that the state pension rises annually by either 2.5 per cent, consumer price index (CPI) inflation or average earnings growth, whichever is highest. This protects pensioners from losing purchasing power as prices rise, and while it was temporarily paused during the COVID pandemic, it has been reinstated.

Interestingly, the state pension has been increasing at a faster rate than many other benefits for working-age people. However, one potential issue is that with the state pension currently paying £11,502 a year, it's getting close to the personal tax allowance of £12,570 (as we covered in Part 2). This means that some pensioners could end up paying income tax on their state pension. While they don't pay national insurance contributions, income tax still applies if their total income exceeds the personal allowance.

New vs. old state pension

I've referred to the state pension so far as 'the state pension' however, there is a new and an old state pension. The new state pension was introduced in 2016 and applies to men born after 5 April 1951 and women born after 5 April 1953. If you were born before these dates, you're on the old state pension system.

The old state pension is a bit more complicated. It has two parts: the basic state pension and an additional element known as the state earnings-related pension scheme (SERPS). The basic state pension is a flat rate, but the additional part is based on your earnings over your working life, meaning the more you earned, the more you can get.

The new state pension simplifies things. It's now a flat rate for everyone, provided you have made 35 years of national insurance contributions. There's no extra bit based on earnings anymore, just the flat weekly rate that everyone who qualifies will get. If you haven't hit the full 35 years, your state pension will be reduced pro-portionally. If you have between 10 and 35 years of contributions, it's done on a percentage basis, so if, for example, you have 11 years, you'll get 11/35ths of the full state pension.

If you are a low-income pensioner and for any reason you haven't managed to accrue qualifying years to get the state pension, you can get pension credits, which would step in as a back-up and entitle you to not only the benefit but also social tariffs and fuel payments.

Many will hit the 35-year mark with ease, but you can check if you have any missing years on the gov.uk 'Check your State Pension forecast' tool; it will show you all the years you've accrued and if there are any missing. A full state pension is currently £230.25 a week, so if you're forecasted less, there is something you can do about it.

Let's say you went abroad for an extended period of time or took a career break where you weren't getting any other benefits like child benefit or universal credit (which do give you those years even if you're not 'working' – the irony is not lost on me that if you're on child benefit you are most definitely working as a parent/grandparent, just not in the eyes of the government).

The good news is that you can buy back missing years, going back six tax years. There are different rates depending on whether you were employed (Class 3 contributions) or self-employed (Class 2 contributions) in the relevant year.

People still in work often ask me if, having made nine years of contributions, they should buy more national insurance years.

In most cases, you don't really need to. If you are not anywhere near retirement, I would advise caution; don't buy years just in case, because if you buy them, they can never be refunded.

There are also some situations where you don't have to pay for the extra years, or have partial years that can be completed for a reduced payment.

And what if you've contributed more than 35 years? Can you stop paying national insurance?

No. Whether you have completed 35 years or not, if you are still eligible to pay national insurance, which means you're not at retirement age just yet, you will still have to contribute. The only people that don't pay national insurance are those that have hit the state pension age, which is currently 66, but that is likely to keep rising.

For many, the state pension is a blessing, and the big question is whether it will be there for future generations; there are so many unknowns, and the main point to repeat is that it is a benefit, not a given. There is space to adjust, and for that reason, other retirement pensions need to be reviewed from a wealth and financial planning perspective.

Workplace pensions

A private workplace pension, unlike the state pension, is not controlled by the government but by you, set up by you and your employer.

You have a pension allowance, which is currently £60,000 a year, or your total gross income (TGI), whichever is lower. This means you can contribute up to £60k (or TGI) into your pension each year tax-free.

The auto-enrolment scheme was introduced in the UK in 2012. All adults above the age of 22 and earning more than £10k a year should be automatically opted into a workplace pension; if you fear you haven't been, contact your HR team. Over 90 per cent of employees now contribute to a workplace pension.

There are two main types of workplace pension: defined benefit pensions and defined contribution pensions.

The defined benefit pension is more or less extinct now. These pensions were also called 'final salary' pensions, where you were guaranteed a certain amount for life. Your employer held all the risk, and while you might have contributed because you were guaranteed a certain amount if you didn't hit that, it wasn't your problem.

These pensions cost the businesses a lot of money. Pensions would sometimes cost more than individual salaries and would need to be paid out after the employee was no longer contributing to the function or productivity of their company which is why they've been phased out.

The most common and well-known is the defined contributions pension. You hold the risk, the pension holder, and what you put in is what you get out.

Your employer puts in a minimum of 3 per cent, and you put in a minimum of 5 per cent; some employers will contribute more than this and let you match up to a higher amount i.e. they will put in 8 per cent if you do.

If you opt out, your employer does not have to contribute, and your pension pot will therefore not be growing.

If you put in just the 5 per cent when they contribute to 8 per cent, you're looking at a contribution of 8 per cent to your pension vs. 16 per cent with the matching scheme. Never leave money that is rightfully yours on the table. That can double the amount in your pension scheme at retirement. We're in the last part of the book about building wealth, and these are some of the chunkiest sums of money we're putting away for you in the future. Don't be too short-term with your mindset.

Pensions are investments

If you are a pension holder, you are an investor; the pension money gets put into a fund, which we covered in Chapter 13, and throughout your life it is invested to try and provide you with a larger pot when you hit retirement than you contributed.

Many of these pensions are 'lifestyle pensions', which means that as you get older, the pots your pensions are invested into get less risky to account for you getting close to retirement and, therefore, wanting to take less risk.

When your pension is invested for you, it goes into a standard fund; this is a fund that your employer picks out to suit everyone. Everyone. Have you ever tried to suit a range of people from 22 to 66 and get it right with anything? No. So these standard funds probably aren't working for you either; we've discussed lifestyle, yes where your fund might lower the risk appetite as you get older, but the standard fund might be lowering your risk already in your 20s because it's the same fund 45-year-old Sally in HR also has her pension in.

You do have a say, and it's important to ensure your fund aligns with your risk appetite. Could you take more risks and, therefore, get more rewards? The increased risk when you're younger could look like thousands of pounds more come retirement.

There is one explanation I hear often from young people choosing to opt out of their workplace pension, and I don't disagree entirely with it. 'I'm not opting into a workplace pension because I'm going to invest the money myself. Yes, I don't get the tax breaks, but I also don't like how the pensions are being invested on my behalf and investing myself means I have more control.'

They are right. Did you know your private pension money gets invested by the government and pension providers?

Pensions aren't always invested in the best interests of the pension holder.

Can I change where my pension is being invested?

Yes, it is your pension and investment pot, and many will be put into default funds that are cost-effective and easier for the pension provider and your employer. You do have options; you don't have to come out of a pension altogether.

You can hold your pension provider to account. Your pension provider should have the top ten holdings on their website, and a listing of the funds your pension is invested in, and this should be updated quarterly.

If you can't find this information, email them and ask about the risk profile of your pension as well as where it's all invested.

Especially if you're younger, you might decide to take more risks, and the 'default' funds are not always as risky as you could be willing to take.

The top tens tend to look very similar regardless of the

provider. When you have this information, you can contact your provider and start the process of moving your money or even start a conversation about consolidation.

Consolidating pensions

This is the big question when it comes to pensions. We live in a society now where we have multiple jobs, even within our first few years out of education, and this means picking up possible multiple pension pots.

Here are the advantages of consolidation:

1. Some pension providers will only give you access to certain funds if you have over a certain amount, so if you combine, you may have more in the pot to, therefore, put into lucrative investments.
2. Administrative ease: this is a two-point pro. First up, consolidating into one means you know exactly where everything is – you can track this more easily. Secondly, whenever you move home, you need to let your pension provider know, and having fewer pensions means fewer people to tell.
3. It can save you money – every pension provider charges you some kind of fee like a standard flat fee, a percentage of what your pension is worth, or even both. If you have five

different pots, why pay fees across five or pay it just once.

And here are the disadvantages:

1. By keeping them separate, you diversify your risk – we know pensions are investments, and the pots differ in return depending on where it's being held.
2. Consolidating them can come with its own set of fees – pension providers sadly don't let you just drain one account and send it somewhere else. They may charge you a changeover fee.
3. Some older pension plans may offer guaranteed annuity rates, which could be more favourable than current market rates. Consolidating pensions might mean losing these valuable guarantees.

Workplace pensions are not the only form of private pension; as we discussed, these workplace pensions are invested on your behalf, and yes, you can get involved and change the investments or even providers. But there are other options, one of which is a SIPP.

SIPPs (self-invested personal pensions)

self-invested personal pensions, or SIPPs, are increasingly popular among individuals who want more control

over their retirement savings. They are the most personalised of the pension options but often the one
we forget about. Remember the £60,000 annual allowance we talked about at the start of this discussion on
private pensions? This is a limit per person across all
your pensions. So, if you're approaching that threshold
and still want to maximise your tax-efficient savings,
SIPPs might be the way forward.

SIPPs are perfect for those who like to be in control
as well as those confident in making their own investment decisions. Unlike traditional workplace pensions,
which often restrict you to a limited set of risk profiles
and funds, SIPPs offer more choices. They give you the
option to invest in things like bonds, individual shares
and commodities.

With a workplace pension, the big driver in the title is
a workplace; if you're employed, you have an employer
whose responsibility it is to set you up with a pension.
If you are self-employed, SIPPs can be a great option
for your retirement planning. With a SIPP, you can open
and manage your pension independently, contributing as
much or as little as you wish, up to the annual allowance.

One of the big advantages of SIPPs is the tax relief.
These are 'relief at source' schemes, meaning that contributions automatically receive basic-rate tax relief.
For example, if you contribute £800, it's automatically
topped up to £1,000 in your SIPP. If you're a higher-
or additional-rate taxpayer, you can claim the extra tax
relief through your self-assessment tax return. Many

people overlook this step and miss out on substantial additional tax benefits, so it's important to stay on top of it.

Remember, though, this is a pension, not an investment pot like a stocks and shares ISA, so it does come with the restriction on when you can access the money – but this is great when you're building wealth for the future, and for riding the waves of the market.

While SIPPs offer a high degree of flexibility and control, they're not for everyone. The breadth of investment options can be overwhelming, and poor investment choices can lead to losses.

Moreover, SIPPs often come with higher fees than standard workplace pensions due to the greater range of services and investment options. It's important to weigh these costs against the potential benefits to determine if a SIPP is the right choice for you.

How do you access your pension?

Taking out your money from SIPPs, as well as state and workplace pensions, is different across the board.

We can't talk about pensions and not talk about the age of our population. It has been steadily rising. The ONS (Office of National Statistics) releases population statistics and estimates. In 1972, out of every 100 people, one was aged 85 or over, and 13 were between 65 and 84. The fraction in the oldest group has since increased to nearly 3 per cent by 2022, while the fraction aged between 65 and 84 has hit 17 per cent. This is a much older country than it was 50 years ago.

The current private pension age is 55 for workplace pensions and SIPPs. It is expected to rise to 57 by 2028 and will keep rising; retiring at 55 for many people just isn't an option anymore. You can delay starting to take down your pension, but many people don't retire purely because there's not enough in their pension to start taking it.

Currently, the state pension age is set at 66, but it is scheduled to rise to 67 between 2026 and 2028. This change has been anticipated for some time as part of the government's efforts to align the pension age with increasing life expectancy and the economic demands of an ageing population. Most governments sit on their hands when it comes to adjusting this age because it will be very unpopular.

What you need to do is review your state pension forecast; this will tell you when you're likely to receive and be eligible for the state pension. You can get access to this via the gov.uk website's 'Check your State Pension forecast' tool, and you can monitor this throughout your career to help with your retirement planning.

Keep an eye on the age change; as we said above, there is going to be a change, as unexpected age changes can mean you'll be thousands of pounds worse off.

If you find that your state pension age will be later than expected, plan for how you will manage any income gaps. This might involve working longer, drawing on private pension savings or adjusting your lifestyle to accommodate a delayed pension.

Private pension

When it comes to pensions, particularly private pensions, SIPPs and workplace pensions, there are a few key tax rules you need to be aware of, especially as you approach retirement age. One important rule that used to exist was the lifetime allowance, which capped the amount you could save in your pension without facing additional tax. However, the lifetime allowance has been abolished. But don't think you're off the hook just yet – there's still an annual allowance.

The annual allowance is now set at £60,000 or your gross income (whichever is lower). If you contribute more than that to your pension in a single tax year, you'll be taxed on the excess contributions.

When you reach retirement age, you've got two main ways of drawing down your pension:

1. The 25 per cent lump sum: You can take 25 per cent of your total pension pot tax-free, up to a maximum of £268,275 (unless you have a protected allowance). This can be a nice upfront boost, but it also means you'll be left with 75 per cent of your pension to be handled differently.

2. The rest (75 per cent): The remaining 75 per
   cent can either be taken all at once – though
   it will be taxed – or spread out over time as an
   annuity, where you draw down a fixed amount
   each year.

What if I need the money before I turn 55?

There are two scenarios where you can access your
pension before the age of 55, but they come with
significant drawbacks:

1. Early withdrawal penalty: If you try to access
   your pension early, you'll face a hefty penalty
   of 55 per cent on the amount you withdraw.
   This option is rarely recommended due to the
   high cost.
2. Terminal illness: If you're diagnosed with a
   terminal illness, the government allows you
   to access your pension early without the same
   penalty, giving you access to your savings when
   you need it most.

What if I've lost a workplace pension?

This is totally fair, given how many workplace pensions
many have throughout their working career. So, there is
a free government tracing service that can help you track
down your old pensions.

On gov.uk there is a tool that allows you to 'Find

pension contact details'; enter the name of your employer and the date you worked there. It will then tell you the pension provider they used that time. You contact that pension provider with your details, and they should be able to tell you how much is in the pot and where it is being invested.

If you've forgotten the name of your old employer, it can make things trickier, but with some effort, there are still ways to dig into your work history and locate those forgotten pensions.

SIPPs

Like the workplace pension, you can access this at 55 (rising to 57 by 2028), but you do have the option to leave it there until you're ready, of course.

When you decide to access your SIPP, you have several options for withdrawing funds in a tax-efficient manner. The most common approach is to take up to 25 per cent of your pension pot as a tax-free lump sum, with the remaining 75 per cent accessible as taxable income.

You can spread your 75 per cent withdrawals over many tax years, keeping below the personal allowance bands we've spoken about. Additionally, you might consider using a drawdown strategy, where your remaining funds stay invested, potentially growing over time and providing you with a steady income stream.

One of the biggest advantages of pensions is that any

money left in your pension could be passed on to your beneficiaries completely tax-free, making pensions one of the most efficient ways to transfer wealth, especially if you've built up a substantial pension pot and don't need to access all of it during your lifetime. However, this is set to change in the next few years, pensions will no longer be fully exempt from inheritance tax (IHT), meaning they may no longer offer the same tax advantages when passed on to beneficiaries.

But there's an important detail to remember: even if you've written a will outlining who should inherit your assets, that doesn't automatically include your pension. To ensure your pension goes to the right person, you need to fill out an expression of wishes form, which tells your pension provider who you'd like the money to go to in the event of your death.

If you forget to complete or update this form, your pension could end up going to someone you no longer have a relationship with, or it could cause unnecessary delays in getting the money to your intended beneficiaries. Make sure this form is filled out and kept up to date to avoid any issues later on.

As we've explored in this chapter, understanding pensions is crucial for securing your financial future. From the state pension and its intricacies, including the new vs. old systems and the triple lock agreement, to the various private pension options like workplace pensions and SIPPs, we've covered the essentials you need to know. We also delved into the importance of checking your contributions, considering the tax benefits, and even the potential for your pension to play a significant role in inheritance planning. As we wrap up our discussion on pensions, it's clear that while these tools are vital for long-term financial security, they are just one piece of the wealth-building puzzle.

In the last chapter, we'll shift our focus to other wealth-building strategies, exploring how you can invest in yourself, create passive income streams and leverage these methods to further enhance your financial well-being. These approaches will complement what you've learned about pensions and provide you with a broader toolkit for achieving your financial goals. Let's continue this journey toward financial empowerment by looking at the diverse ways you can build and sustain wealth beyond traditional retirement planning.

THINGS YOU NEED TO REMEMBER:

- There is an eligibility for the state pension. You need to have made at least 10 years of national insurance contributions to be eligible for the state pension, and 35 years to receive the full state pension.

- Private and state pensions are different, and within private, there are workplace pensions and SIPPs.

- If you plan to pass your pension along to someone after your death, you have to make sure you've filled in an expression of wishes form.

15. How to Invest in Yourself

As we come to the final chapter, it's time to focus on what I believe has the biggest impact on your financial success: investing in yourself. We've covered everything from tax codes to mortgages, pensions to credit cards, but the most valuable investment you'll ever make isn't found in stocks or savings, it's in levelling up your own knowledge, skills and confidence.

This book has been about building your financial toolkit, helping you feel in control of your money and giving you the insight to make the best choices for you. You don't need to rely solely on financial advisors or accountants to lay the foundation for a life of financial stability and growth. Instead, by investing in yourself, you're equipping future you to set and reach your financial goals on your terms.

It's easy to think of finance as something complex, but by now, I hope you see it differently. Finance doesn't actually have to be complicated. By taking ownership of your learning, you've already taken the biggest step towards building a strong financial future. This chapter is about guiding you to keep that momentum going.

Recognising your worth

When it comes to investing in yourself, start with recognising your own worth. Not just your net worth, the financial snapshot of what you own versus what you owe, but your personal worth. Your self-worth isn't about numbers, but about confidence, self-belief and the mindset you bring to your goals.

Financially, knowing your net worth gives you a clear idea of where you stand and where you'd like to go. It's a powerful way to see what you've built and how much more you can achieve. But beyond the numbers, knowing your *personal* worth helps you set boundaries, negotiate better and make financial choices that genuinely align with your values. Money is a tool to help you achieve what matters most to you, but it's your worth, your confidence and your self-respect that guides how you use it.

I get asked, 'Abi how do I work out my net worth?' So let's take Elliot; he has a car worth £5k, £10k in savings and owes about £3k in student loans. Therefore his total assets would come to £15k (£5k car and £10k savings) and then his liabilities would be the £3k student loan.

So his net worth would be £15,000 − £3,000 = £12,000.

The idea is to increase your assets and decrease your liabilities over time. Building a positive net worth provides a financial cushion, while consistently growing it is a sign of progress.

Levelling up your income

When you start a new job, ask for more money right from the get-go. Think of it this way: the offer is on the table because they want *you*, and in this moment, you hold the power to negotiate. Even if the thought of it feels intimidating, remember, the worst they can say is 'no'. And if they do, you still have the job you were excited about.

Take my friend Sophie, for example. I was with her when she got an offer, and I encouraged her to push for more. She was nervous, but after a deep breath and a bit of courage, she did it; she asked for more. To her surprise, they agreed, just like that. Sophie got the full amount she asked for, and her confidence skyrocketed. I wasn't shocked, though. Employers often have some leeway in the budget for the right candidate, so why shouldn't that be you? The key is learning to ask.

Now, maybe you've been in your role for a while and are ready to ask for a raise. Here's how you can approach it effectively:

1. Know your value: Before you even start the conversation, research your role and the industry standards. Know what the market pays for someone with your skills and experience.
2. Document your achievements: Be ready to show how you've added value to the company.

Did you bring in new clients, increase revenue or make a process more efficient? Have examples and numbers to back it up. I would recommend keeping a 'proud of me' document on your computer that you keep these bits in.

3. Be clear and confident: When you have the meeting, be straightforward. Explain the value you bring and why you deserve a raise. Don't demand; make it a discussion.

4. Be ready to negotiate: Even if your employer can't give you exactly what you ask for, be open to negotiating other benefits like bonuses, more holiday time or opportunities for growth.

Great job on securing that raise! But don't stop there. Real, lasting financial growth often comes from continuous personal development. Just as you advocated for a pay increase, now's the time to start investing in skills that will keep pushing your income upward. Upskilling, especially in high-demand areas like technology and communication, future-proofs your career and makes you more valuable in any role. Consider it a way to build career resilience, positioning yourself not just for job security but also for the exciting roles that pay well and keep you evolving.

In today's fast-moving world, skills in technology are gold. Whether it's learning to code, understanding data analysis, or even mastering digital marketing, these are the skills that businesses are crying out for. Having even a basic grasp of tech makes you more adaptable and puts you ahead of the curve in almost every industry.

Equally important are communication skills. You can be the best at what you do, but if you can't articulate your value or build relationships, you're limiting yourself. Improving how you communicate, whether it's in meetings, presentations or just everyday conversations, can open doors and help you stand out in your field.

And then there's entrepreneurship. Even if you don't want to start your own business, thinking like an entrepreneur gives you a mindset of problem-solving, innovation and opportunity-seeking. These are traits that employers value and are skills you can apply anywhere to increase your impact and income.

Building your network and personal brand

Investing in yourself also means expanding your network and cultivating a personal brand. Networking isn't just about collecting business cards, it's about building meaningful relationships that support your career, introduce you to new opportunities and provide mentorship. Your network is a unique source of inspiration, guidance and career growth, so invest time in it.

Finally, don't underestimate the power of personal branding. Your personal brand is how people perceive you, and it's incredibly valuable. Whether it's through your social media presence, speaking at events or simply becoming known as the go-to person in your field, investing in your personal brand can open doors you didn't even know existed.

I do think there's a layer before this as well, and that's how you're perceived in your friendship group and family; something I've had to relearn a few times is that pushing yourself too far pushes friends away because they think you don't care. When, in reality, you do, so in the chase for financial success, don't let your personality and your friendships fall by the wayside.

The power of teaching

Teaching is my passion, and it's been the driving force behind my work on closing the gender pay gap and promoting financial literacy. When I left my stable job to pursue teaching finance in schools, I knew that true change starts with the next generation. I remember my first day, standing in front of more than 200 students, feeling energised as I watched understanding dawn on their faces. These moments reminded me of the power and importance of financial education.

Teaching doesn't have to mean standing in a classroom; sometimes, it's as simple as sharing what you know with the people around you. Whether it's explaining tax codes to your flatmate or breaking down a payslip for your niece, small conversations can make a world of difference. In finance, if you can explain a concept simply, you've mastered it. And explaining it to someone else? That's the next level.

Teaching is hard work. It's why I believe teachers deserve the utmost respect. But it's worth it. When you teach someone else, you don't just deepen your understanding; you contribute to a ripple effect of knowledge. Financial literacy isn't reserved for the elite, it's a right for everyone. The more we share, the more we build a fairer, financially empowered world.

Teaching across ages: financial literacy for every stage

When teaching finance, think about the ages you're speaking to:

- Ages 0–7: Start lightly. This is when money mindsets are formed, so be mindful of your words and actions around money.
- Ages 8–12: Make it hands-on. Show them how a card works or where money goes when you buy something. Explain the basics in everyday moments.
- Ages 13–18: This is a crucial stage. Engage teens by talking about investing, understanding a payslip or avoiding debt traps. Teach them what you wish you'd known at their age.
- Everyone else: Be bold. Take any lesson from this book and explain it to someone else; it's

how we build a world of financially aware individuals.

My ultimate goal is a world where everyone is financially literate, confident and equipped to advocate for themselves. But I can't do it alone. You are part of this journey, one conversation at a time. When we teach, we don't just close gaps, we erase them.

That said, while sharing knowledge and learnings with your friends is invaluable, it's crucial to acknowledge when a professional is needed. The whole aim of this book is to give you tools, but sadly it cannot turn you into an accountant or financial advisor. At any point when it becomes overwhelming please reach out to a qualified professional.

THINGS YOU NEED TO REMEMBER:

- Invest in your skills, and these include networking and personal branding.

- You truly understand something when you can teach it. Sharing your financial knowledge with others solidifies your own understanding and helps spread financial literacy.

- Start by sharing what you've learned with friends, family or colleagues. Every conversation about money can help close the knowledge gap and empower others.

What to do now?

We started this journey by looking inwards, unpacking the habits we've picked up over the years – some good, some not so good – and realising how often we've been misinformed or left in the dark about money. We've seen how habits and attitudes you learned from an early age impact how you approach money now, but it's not a trap; you can change. It's fully OK to stand up and say, 'Nope, you know what? I've read the entire length of *The Money Manual.* I've got this; I know what I need, and I'm smashing it.'

As we went further into the more technical parts of the book, you might have read certain parts and thought, *Wait, that's not what I was told!* And that's because people, often with the best intentions, can be constantly and confidently wrong about finance. There are creators with zero knowledge, teachers who have one viewpoint of the world, and even parents who will confidently tell you that one type of credit card is best because it may have been back when they applied. With that in mind, this book isn't just a guide for today. It's a resource, a tool you can return to when life's big (and small) money moments arise. Whether it's decoding your next payslip, understanding how to invest for the first time, or figuring out how to best save for a rainy day, *The Money Manual* is your financial playbook.

But let's take this one step further. The knowledge

you've gained isn't just about you; it has the potential to create a ripple effect. As you become more financially literate, you'll naturally start sharing this knowledge. You'll talk to friends, family, even strangers and pass on these lessons. And that's how change happens: one conversation at a time. We create a society where financial knowledge isn't gatekept, and everyone feels empowered to make smart decisions about their money. That ripple effect? It's how we close gaps, whether they're based on gender, income or opportunity, and build a fairer world.

The financial system wasn't designed for you to win. It wasn't built with your best interests at heart, and it thrives on keeping people in the dark. That's why financial education so often comes too late or from people who don't care enough. But with this book, you're ahead of the curve. You're not just another cog in the machine. You're informed, and that gives you power.

So, what's next? Don't let this knowledge sit on a shelf. Use it. Take a proactive approach to your financial life. Whether it's making that call to review your pension, starting a new investment plan, or just taking the time to educate someone else, make sure you're always moving forward.

Lastly, remember that the world of money will keep evolving as markets change, rules shift, and new challenges arise. But now, you've got the foundation to keep up. Keep learning, keep asking questions and, most importantly, keep believing that you have the ability to shape your financial future – because you do.

Further Resources

References

1 Berti, A. E., and A. S. Bombi, *The Child's Construction of Economics* (Cambridge, 1988)

2 Lindsay, Sam, 'BLOG: It's 50 Years since Women Were Allowed to Get a Mortgage on Their Own', 2024 <https://www.yourmoney.com/blog/blog-its-50-years-since-women-were-allowed-to-get-a-mortgage-on-their-own/> [accessed 6 January 2025]

3 Boyce, Lee, 'Why You're Ten Times More Likely to Win £100,000 on Premium Bonds – But Less Likely to Win £1m: Find out YOUR Odds after Major Changes to Payouts', This Is Money, 2023 <https://www.thisismoney.co.uk/money/saving/article-11986395/Why-youre-ten-times-likely-win-100-000-Premium-Bonds.html> [accessed 6 January 2025]

4 Lewis, Paul, 'The Average Premium Bond Saver Has To Wait 16 Years To Win. I'm Not That Patient', The I Paper, 2023 <https://inews.co.uk/inews-lifestyle/money/paul-lewis-premium-bond-savers-not-patient-2572862> [accessed 6 January 2025]

Acknowledgements

First and foremost, a huge thank you to my editor, Géraldine, and the team at Penguin Random House UK and Ebury for believing in this book, even when I sent voice notes in various states of panic. Your patience, wisdom, and ability to make my ramblings sound coherent have been nothing short of miraculous.

To my family and friends thank you for putting up with me, for enduring my ability to turn *any* conversation into a conversation about your finances (and still inviting me to things), and for being there for every milestone in my life. Your support means everything, even if some of you still refuse to read your own payslips.

Mum, Dad, Brother . . . do I just keep listing people here? I feel like I'm giving an acceptance speech at the Oscars. If you know you should be in here, consider yourself thanked.

To my newest family, every single person who has ever watched one of my videos on that tiny, chaotic, wonderful corner of the internet called social media, this book exists because of you. Your questions, your struggles, your wins, and even your *mildly concerning* DMs inspired every chapter.

And finally, to you – yes, you – holding this book right now. Thank you for trusting me to help you on your financial journey. I hope this makes you feel more confident, less overwhelmed, and slightly smug when you finally understand what the MPC do.

Index

About the Author

Abigail Foster is a qualified chartered accountant and the founder of Elent, a platform and accompanying app that provides you with educational resources and guidance on how to achieve the financial freedom and literacy you missed out on at school.

Beyond this, Abigail is a leading financial expert, appearing frequently on LBC, Sky News, *This Morning* and Channel 5. She is also an advocate for financial education to be brought into the school curriculum, interviewing and pressing key policymakers including ex-prime minister Rishi Sunak and Governor of the Bank of England, Andrew Bailey.

Abigail has a large social media community with over 200k followers on Instagram and TikTok, where she delivers engaging personal finance education. *The Money Manual* is her first book.